Herrmann Fick

Life and deeds of Dr. Martin Luther

Herrmann Fick

Life and deeds of Dr. Martin Luther

ISBN/EAN: 9783337127176

Printed in Europe, USA, Canada, Australia, Japan

Cover: Foto ©ninafisch / pixelio.de

More available books at **www.hansebooks.com**

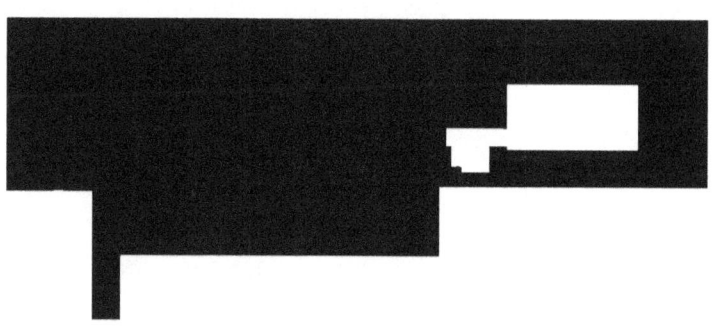

1869.

Entered, according to Act of Congress, in the year 1868,
BY J. A. SCHULZE,
in the Clerk's Office of the District Court of the United States for the Southern District of Ohio.

PREFACE.

In these times it is becoming more and more a necessity for Ev. Lutherans to make themselves acquainted with the history of Luther's life. The Papists assail him with constantly increasing vehemence, and impute to him the grossest sins. Even some who call themselves Protestants make the gravest charges against him. Formerly the whole Ev. Lutheran Church was unanimous in the conviction, that Luther was the divinely commissioned Reformer of the Church and the herald of divine truth. But now the number of those is on the increase, even in the Ev. Lutheran Church, who deny him this honor. They maintain, of course without the least proof, that he erred in various articles of faith, and do not hesitate to dispute his vocation as a Reformer. How easily, under such circumstances, may not even faithful Lutherans be led to waver in their faith, especially when great scholars and distinguished theologians utter such censures. To defend ourselves successfully against these false accusations we have no better means than that of a more intimate acquaintance with his writings and his life.

We hope, therefore, to meet a general want of our Church in this small volume. May God graciously own it as a means to lead us the more joyfully to thank Him for what we possess in Luther. When we contemplate his history, the wonderful ways in which he was led, and the glorious success of his work, we see most clearly that he was called by God himself to be the deliverer and restorer of His Church, and that as such he was divinely authenticated and sealed. When we examine his doctrine we find that it harmonizes perfectly with the Holy Scriptures, so that he preached nothing but the pure word of God. When we view his gifts we must confess that, since the times of the apostles, no one possessed such a full measure of the Spirit, of wisdom, and of the knowledge of the Lord, as Luther. When we look, finally, upon his life we find a shining example of Christian virtues. All this furnishes abundant evidence that Luther had a divine call to reform the Church.

But there is another motive for the earnest contemplation of Luther's life. For our times Luther is a salutary example : for he not only confessed with his lips that the Holy Scriptures are the highest and only rule in matters of faith, but in this confession he showed himself to be thoroughly in earnest. He took captive every thought to the obedience of Christ. He submitted in a child-like spirit to the word of God, and received it humbly in its literal meaning and as interpreted by itself. Therefore he rejected every doctrine which contradicts the divine word, however acceptable it might seem to his natural reason. He stood upon the pure, uncorrupted word of God alone ; this alone he believed, taught and confessed. Hence his good conscience, his deep joy of faith, and his pure knowledge of God. He was conscious that he sought only God's truth and glory. Hence also the powerful effect of his preaching. For the Gospel, which he again proclaimed in its purity, manifested its glorious divine power in his hearers and converted thousands, yea, whole nations, from the darkness of Romanism to the living God.

Our times, on the other hand, are inundated with false human doctrines as with a flood.

Nearly every year adds to the number of new religions. The majority fabricate their own religion, and many set forth their peculiar notions and whims as new revelations, to say nothing of the fools who, in their satanic infatuation, proclaim it as the highest wisdom to believe in no God at all. But what is saddest of all is that so many, who still extol the Bible as the word of God, in so many points depart from it, and follow the false opinions of men in preference to the blessed and unchangable utterances of the God of truth.

Of what avail are all these futile doctrines of men? They are vain cobwebs, and nothing more. Though they appear ever so beautiful and ingenious, they are but shining bubbles which soon must burst. Wo to the unhappy mortals who put their trust in them; temporal and eternal ruin is their doom.

Luther himself declares that he adhered to the command of God, Matt. xvii, 5: "This is my beloved Son, in whom I am well pleased; hear ye him," and that thus he was preserved in the true faith, otherwise he would, during his life, have been constrained to embrace a score of different faiths. Let us follow his example; beware of the traditions of men; accept the word of God as the only ground of our salvation; and remain steadfast in this unto our end. Then, though the last storms should burst upon us, we shall not fall.— Founded upon the eternal rock of God's word, we rest in the hand of the Almighty, out of which nothing shall be able to wrest us.

To all Lutherans in North America, in sincere love, be then this humble tribute dedicated and commended. May this little book serve, by the grace of God, to instruct and edify those of maturer years and strengthen them in their faith. May it be welcomed in the school as a book of instruction to more advanced youth. It would undoubtedly be of great benefit to children if in the schools they were made acquainted with the history of Luther's life, and were thus early taught to love the pure doctrine of our Church. May God in mercy richly bless this book, though it is written in much weakness, to all who read it: it is His glory to choose that which is weak and despised in this world. 1 Cor. i, 27, 28. To Him be glory and honor and thanks and praise, in time and in eternity, through Jesus Christ, His dear Son, our Lord and Savior. Amen.

INDEX.

I.	Prophecies concerning the Antichrist and concerning Dr. Luther .... page	1
II.	Luther's Birth and Childhood........................	8
III.	Luther at School in Magdeburg.....................	14
IV.	Luther at School in Eisenach........................	18
V.	Luther studies at Erfurt	21
VI.	Luther becomes a Monk	26
VII.	Luther's monastic Labor	31
VIII.	Luther's Ordination as Priest......................	37
IX.	Luther's Conflicts in the Cloister...................	41
X.	How Luther was consoled in the Cloister.........	46
XI.	Luther is called to Wittenberg	51
XII.	Luther's Pilgrimage to Rome........................	55
XIII.	Luther becomes Doctor of the Holy Scriptures.	63
XIV.	Tetzel's scandalous Indulgence traffic.............	70
XV.	The Elector's prophetic Dream of Luther.........	80
XVI.	Luther's ninety-five Theses.—Beginning of the Reformation	84
XVII.	Negotiations with Cajetan and Miltitz............	87
XVIII.	The Leipzig Disputation...........................	96
XIX.	Luther burns the papal Bull.......................	97
XX.	Luther goes to Worms...............................	100
XXI.	Luther at the Diet	104
XXII.	Luther at the Wartburg	112
XXIII.	Luther returns to Wittenberg.....................	116
XXIV.	The Peasant war	120
XXV.	Luther's Marriage	124
XXVI.	The Marburg Conference...........................	128
XXVII.	The Presentation of the Augsburg Confession..	133
XXVIII.	Reformatory Labors................................	149
XXIX.	The last Years of Luther's Life	161
XXX.	Luther's last Days, Death and Burial............	171

THE
Life and Deeds of Dr. Martin Luther.

CHAPTER I.
PROPHECIES CONCERNING THE ANTICHRIST AND CONCERNING DR. LUTHER.

Our Lord Jesus Christ, since the times of the apostles, has done many great and wonderful works. But the most glorious of these is undoubtedly the Reformation of the Church, which He accomplished through His chosen instrument, Dr. Martin Luther. For through him He purified the doctrine from all error and idolatry, and delivered His people from the terrible tyranny of the Romish papacy.

But when God designs to perform a great work He usually makes a previous announcement of it to His believers. He not only foretells the plagues and punishments which shall befall them, but also the glorious aid and deliverance which He purposes to send them. This is true also in the times of the New Testament, and we cannot sufficiently thank God for His grace. If the papacy, with its horrible abominations, had sprung up without any prophecy of it in the Scriptures, believers

1*

might easily have been led astray by it. If no comfort and assistance had been promised them, they would not have had such cheerfulness of faith in the persecutions and sufferings which they were called to endure, for Jesus' sake, at the hands of the pope. And if God had not so plainly predicted the Reformation effected through Dr. Luther, we could not so confidently confess it to be God's own work, which He purposed from eternity, and which he gloriously accomplished in its time.

Both in the Old and the New Testament God portrays the Romish Antichrist and his kingdom in the most vivid colors. The prophet Daniel says of him, vii, 25: "He shall speak great words against the Most High, and shall wear out the saints of the Most High, and think to change times and laws." More in detail he speaks of him in chapter xi, where he says, v. 31—38: "And the king shall do according to his will; and he shall exalt himself, and magnify himself above every god, and shall speak marvellous things against the God of gods, and shall prosper till the indignation be accomplished: for that, that is determined, shall be done. Neither shall he regard the God of his fathers, nor the desire of women, (matrimony,) nor regard any god: for he shall magnify himself above all. But in his estate shall he honor the god of forces (the idol of the mass): and a god of whom his fathers knew not shall he honor with gold and silver, and with precious stones and pleasant things." This the apostle more fully explains in 2 Thess. 2, 3—4: "Let no man deceive you by any means, for that day (the day of judgment) shall not come, except there come a falling away first and that man of sin be revealed, the son of perdition; who opposeth and exalteth himself above all that is called God, or that is worshipped; so that he as God sitteth in the temple of God showing himself that he is God." The doctrines of devils which the Antichrist with his adherents shall introduce, are mentioned by St. Paul in 1 Tim. iv, 1—3: "Now the Spirit speaketh expressly, that in the latter times some shall depart from the faith, giving heed to seducing spirits and doctrines of devils; speaking lies in hypocrisy; having their conscience seared with a hot iron; forbidding to marry, and commanding to abstain from meats, which God hath created to be received with thanksgiving of them which believe and know the truth." And St. John thus describes the kingdom of Antichrist, in Rev. xvii, 3—6: "And I saw a woman sit upon a scarlet beast, full of names of blasphemy, having seven heads and ten horns. And the woman was arrayed in purple and scarlet color, and decked with gold and precious stones and pearls, having a golden cup in her hand full of abominations and filthiness of her fornication; and upon her forehead was a name written, Mystery, Babylon the Great, the Mother of Harlots and Abominations of the earth. And I saw the woman drunken with the blood of the saints, and with the blood of the martyrs of Jesus."

This kingdom of Antichrist will continue until the day of judgment, as St. Paul testifies, 2 Thess. ii, 8 : "Whom the Lord shall consume with the spirit of His mouth, and shall destroy with the brightness of His coming." But the Scriptures at the same time prophesy that God shall triumphantly deliver His Church from the captivity of the Romish Antichrist. Daniel predicts, xi, 44, that "tidings out of the east and out of the north shall trouble him." This took place in the time of Luther. Through him the tidings of the Gospel again resounded, from the north of Europe, from Germany, through all the world, and brought a deadly terror to the papacy, from which it will never fully recover. But highly important is another prophecy, 2 Thess. ii, 3, 6, 8, which the Holy Ghost thrice repeats and which in v. 8 reads thus: "And then shall that Wicked be revealed." The mystery of Antichristian iniquity consists in this, that the pope, as the mortal enemy of Christ, fiercely persecuted and slew the true Christians, and yet so artfully decked himself with the name and word of Christ, that the world considered him Christ's best friend.. But Luther revealed the Antichrist, that is, exposed or unmasked him. He divested him of his hypocritical halo of holiness, and clearly proved from the word of God that the pope, though externally he seem as holy as the Lamb of God, is internally nothing but Satan. Especially beautiful is the following passage, in which the Holy Spirit describes the work of Luther with great clearness: "And I saw another angel fly in the midst of heaven, having the everlasting Gospel to preach unto them that dwell on the earth, and to every nation, and kindred, and tongue, and people, saying with a loud voice, Fear God and give glory to Him; for the hour of His judgment is come; and worship Him that made heaven, and earth, and the fountains of waters." Rev. xiv, 6—7.

But the voice of prophecy did not cease with the holy apostles. God desired to comfort his saints, who sighed under the terrible oppression of the papacy. Therefore by His Holy Spirit He raised up many who pointed to the approaching Reformation. From the great number of these prophecies we select only the following. *Dante Alighieri*, the greatest poet of Italy, who died in 1421, foretold the year of the Reformation when he sang: "This I plainly see and therefore proclaim it. To give him time, the near stars are secure against opposition and resistance. Then, in 1515, one sent of God will cleave that harlot and that giant that sins with her." In the year 1515, Luther became a Doctor of Theology and was sworn to teach the truth which, two years later, he publicly confessed.

St. *Mechtildis*, in 1350, prophesied: "In Germany fierce conflicts will arise on account of religion. Then the Romish Church will fall from the faith entirely and publicly, which she had already done secretly. But in Germany a pure and persecuted little flock will remain, who shall worship God in piety and purity. God will raise up new Pastors who shall proclaim to the people the sound doctrine of Christ, build up and renew the tottering Church, purify the Christian religion now corrupted by so many errors, and preach against Antichrist. But prior to this the pious will, on account of pure religion, be bitterly persecuted by the Antichrist, the chief adversary of the pure doctrine."

The esteemed martyr *John Huss*, who in 1415 was burned by the papists, said to his enemies, shortly before his death, in allusion to his name, Huss, which, in Bohemian, means goose : "To-day you roast a goose, but after a hundred years a swan shall arise from my ashes, which you will not be able to roast."

Jerome of Prague, the friend of Huss, who also died the martyr's death in 1415, declared to his judges a short time before his execution: "I shall leave a thorn in your hearts, and now cite you before the highest Judge to answer me within a hundred years."

When the German emperor *Sigismund* saw the Reformation undertaken by the Council of Constance dissolved in smoke, he was very sad. Whilst he sought recreation in Pressburg, in Hungary, in 1420, a man of venerable aspect, clothed in priestly apparel, appeared to him in a dream and informed him that the errors of the pope and the priests would be disclosed in future times by learned men who, with the aid of several princes, would reform the Church according to the word of God.

Giralemo Savonarola, who was also burned by the pope in Florence, in 1498, prophesied shortly before his death : "The time will soon come when the abominations and idolatries of the Roman pope will be punished, and a teacher shall be born whom none will be able to resist."

Dr. *John Fleck*, a Franciscan prior, in an address delivered at the dedication of the University of Wittenberg, said that all the world would receive wisdom from this "weiszen Berge," (white mountain.)

In 1516 there was a man in Rostock who was commonly called the prophet. This man cried out before all the churches and other places of the city, that the deliverance of Israel from the Babylonish captivity was at hand and that the people should repent. "Awake, ye priests !" he cried, "from your deep sleep of sin, and repent ! Awake, ye citizens, from your errors and be converted ! Your salvation and freedom are near, O ye saints ! Your destruction is at hand, O ye wicked !" &c. For this he was derided by some, and banished from the city by the authorities.

It was a general report, immediately before the dawn of the Reformation, that a monk, and he a hermit, would reform Christendom. For this God appointed the monk, Luther, who belonged to the Augustinian order, which was also called "the hermits."

CHAPTER II.
Luther's Birth and Childhood.

Luther was born on the 10th of November, 1483, between eleven and twelve o'clock at night, at Eisleben, in the county of Mansfeld. On the following day he was baptized in St. Peter's Church and received the name *Martin*, after the saint to whom the day was dedicated, Bishop Martin of Tours. His parents were *John Luther* and *Margaret*, whose maiden name was *Lindemann*. They were originally from Moehra, a village between Eisenach and Salzungen. Of his ancestors Luther says: "I am the son of a peasant. My father, grandfather, ancestors were all peasants. Afterwards my father removed to Mansfeld and became a miner. Hence I sprang." He came to that place in needy circumstances. "My parents," Luther says, "were at first very poor. My father was a poor hewer, and my mother carried the wood upon her back by which we were raised. They endured many hardships; nowadays people would not submit to them." Still, Luther always remembered the place of his birth with joy. He was accustomed to say: "Haec est Islebia"—here is life, because there he received it. He never ceased to love his native land, and always faithfully sought its welfare.

God, in His goodness, blessed his father's labors in Mansfeld, so that He acquired a house and two furnaces. He also became a councilman and was, on account of his integrity, beloved and esteemed by the old count *Guenther*, and by all honest men. His mother "had many virtues that adorn a good woman. Her fear of God, and her prayerful spirit, were particularly remarked. She was looked upon by all other pious women as a model of virtue and decorum." Both parents taught their son to fear God and abound in good works. The father often prayed aloud and fervently, at the bed-side of the child, that God would give his son grace to remember His holy name and to promote the dissemination of His pure doctrine. Because he loved piety and learning, and also for his son's sake, he treated pious ministers and teachers with much respect and kindness. But the parental discipline was at the same time severe. Luther himself says : "My father once punished me so severely that I ran away, and disliked him until he won me to himself again. My mother at one time chastised me about a trifling nut until the blood came ; and the stern and austere life which she led induced me to flee to a cloister and become a monk. They thought they were doing right and meant it kindly ; they only failed to distinguish dispositions, according to which chastisement must be tempered. Punishment is necessary, but the apple should accompany the rod."

As soon as Martin was able to learn, his pious parents took measures to have him instructed. His father, with earnest prayers, sent him to the Latin school, whither old Nich. Oemler often carried him on his arms. There he studied diligently and soon learned the Ten Commandments, the Creed, the Lord's Prayer ; he also practiced penmanship and studied Donatus, the youth's Grammar, Cisio Janus (a Latin Calender,) and memorized some Christian hymns. This school he attended until his fourteenth year. There also he experienced excessively harsh treatment. His teachers belonged to those "inept schoolmasters," of whom he says that "they often spoil fine talents by their clamoring and storming, their knocks and blows, dealing with children as the jailor deals with thieves." He complains of the "hell and purgatory of the schools, in which we have been tortured about the casuals and the temporals, learning just nothing, with all the chastisement, trembling, fear and misery." "How sorry I am," he says in his epistle to the aldermen, "that I did not read more poets and historians, and that no person taught me them."

In the time of his childhood at Mansfeld occurred also the little event of his school-days, which he narrates in his exposition of Genesis, and upon which he makes some edifying remarks. "When God proves us he permits manifold obstacles to obstruct our path, so that we cannot see His purpose ; as when one amuses himself by playing with a worm, laying a stick or a straw in its way, so that it cannot creep whither it would, but must turn to and fro, and try everywhere and every way to get out of the difficulty. But this play of divine grace and benevolence we do not at first understand, and the benefits and the grace itself, which are shown us, we explain to our terror and destruction. It happens to us as it happened to me once, when I was a little boy, and to my companions, with whom I was collecting the alms by which we were supported in our studies. When we were going around from house to house, at the time when the Church celebrates the birth of Christ, singing in four parts the usual psalms about the child Jesus born in Bethlehem, we came to the house of a peasant, which stood alone at the end of the village. When the peasant heard us singing, he came out and inquired in rough, rustic words, where we were, and said: "Where are you boys?" bringing some sausages along, which he purposed to give us. But we were so terrified at the words that we all ran away ; although we had no good reason to be afraid, since the peasant had the serious intention to give us the sausages, and offered them in good faith. Our hearts had become timid on account of the daily threats and tyranny, which the teachers practiced towards the poor pupils, and were thus the more easily alarmed by such sudden terrors. While we were running away the peasant called us, and we laid aside our fear, went to him, and received the gifts which he offered us." We learn from this, at the same time, how he had to struggle with poverty at Mansfeld, as it is related of him also, that he attended funerals for a penny.

This tyrannical school discipline could only render our Martin shy and timorous. But the religious instruction which he received also tended only to alarm and terrify him still more; for what he learned was mostly nothing but papistic superstition and idolatry. No one taught him to derive comfort from his holy baptism; on the contrary, he says of his teachers: "As soon as we have laid off our infant shoes, the act of baptism scarcely being completed, they deprived us of all again by telling us: O, thou hast long since lost thy baptism and polluted thy baptismal dress with sin; thou must now think about atoning and rendering satisfaction for thy sins, of fasting and praying, of pilgrimages and foundations, until thou hast appeased God and been restored to His grace." Much less did he learn truly to know Christ. "I was accustomed from childhood," he says, "to become pale and terror-stricken when I heard the name of Christ mentioned; for I was not taught to think of him otherwise than as of a rigorous and angry Judge." He was directed to his own merits, rather, and to the intercession of the saints. He remarks upon this : "We were shamefully deceived under the papacy, for Christ was not set before us in His clemency, as He is by the prophets, apostles, and by Christ Himself, but he was represented as terrible, so that we feared him more than we did Moses, and thought that the doctrines of Moses were milder and more benignant than those of Christ. Therefore we knew no better than to think of Christ as an angry Judge, whose wrath we must appease by good works and holy living, and whose grace we must secure by the merits and intercession of the saints. This is not only base lying, and lamentably deceiving poor consciences, but it is also a deep revilement of the grace of God, a denial of Christ's death, resurrection, ascension and all his unspeakable benefits, a defamation and condemnation of the Gospel, and an extirpation of the faith, while nothing but abominations, falsehoods, errors and blasphemies are substituted for it. If this is not darkness I know not what darkness is ; and yet no one perceived it, but all regarded it as the pure truth."

Thus Luther grew up in the darkness of papistic error, and even as a child was compelled to experience its bitterness. Not a drop of grace, not a ray of heavenly truth, refreshed his heart, which was filled with terror on account of Christ's wrath. Therefore he vowed, already in his childhood, to make a pilgrimage to Rome and "become pious" as he, according to a manuscript account, once expressed it when the conversation turned upon his visit to Rome. Thus he had entirely lost Christ whom he had put on in Baptism, and would have been eternally lost if God had called him away in that condition. This he himself confesses when he says: "If God refused to help us until we become grateful, what would have become of me when I was twelve years old?"

CHAPTER III.
LUTHER AT SCHOOL IN MAGDEBURG.

At that time the Latin schools in Saxony were in a tolerably good condition. When, therefore, Martin had reached his fourteenth year, he was, in 1497, sent to the Latin school of the Franciscans at Magdeburg, in company with John Reineck, who ever afterwards remained his good friend. There, like the son of many an honest and wealthy man, he sought his bread by singing at the doors of citizens. What is to become great must begin small, and when children are trained to effeminacy and sumptuousness they suffer for it all their lives.

While there, he was taken with a violent fever, which caused him great distress. Water having been denied him, he suffered much from thirst; and once, on a Friday, when all had gone to Church and left him alone in the house, he crept upon his hands and knees into the kitchen, seized a vessel containing fresh water, drank it with great relish, and returned, in the same way, to his chamber, which, in his feebleness, he could scarcely reach before the members of the household returned. Upon this draught he fell into a profound sleep, and the fever left him. At a later period he observed, with reference to this, that he had been informed by several learned physicians that in such burning fevers a copious draught of cold water diminishes the internal heat, as fire is quenched by water.

Luther relates an example of monastic sanctity, occurring at this period, which made a deep impression upon him. "In my fourteenth year, when I was attending school at Magdeburg, I saw with these eyes a prince of Anhalt, the brother of the provost Adolph, afterwards Bishop of Merseburg, in a monk's cowl begging bread through the wide streets, and bending under the sack, like an ass; but his brother went without a burden, by his side, that the pious prince might alone present to the world the highest example of gray, tonsured sanctity. They had so beguiled him that he also performed every other work of the monastery, like the rest of the monks; and he had, by fasting, watching and mortification, become so reduced that he looked like a skeleton, nothing but skin and bone. He died soon afterward, for he was unable to endure such a rigorous life. In fine, whoever saw him, melted with devotion, and had to be ashamed of his secular calling. I think there are still many in Magdeburg who saw it."

Efforts were made also to represent by pictures, this great priestly sanctity to the people. Luther describes one which must have made a deep impression upon him in his youth. "They painted a large ship, which they called the Holy Christian Church, in which sat no laymen and no kings nor princes, but only the pope with his cardinals and bishops, who occupied the front, under the Holy Spirit, and the priests and monks, who sat with oars on the sides; and thus they sailed away towards heaven. The laity swam in the water about the ship; some were drowning, some drawing themselves to the ship by ropes, which the holy fathers, by grace and by sharing their good works, cast out to them that they might not drown, but be taken along to heaven, clinging to the ship. There was not a pope, cardinal, bishop, priest or monk in the water; nothing but laymen. This picture was a representation and brief summary of their doctrine concerning secular callings; and that it is a fair representation of the doctrine contained in their books they cannot deny. For I also was one of the company that taught such things, believing them in my ignorance. Thus they condemned laymen with their whole order, insomuch that even princes and lords, in the hour of death, had monk's cowls put upon their heads and were buried in them, thus boldly denying Christ and renouncing and despising Baptism and all sacraments, condemning their secular vocation, putting all their trust in the holy cowl and the imputation of the good works of the order, and deriving all their consolation from them, whilst, clinging to their rope and their ship, they ascended to heaven." Once he exhibited a tablet, upon which this picture was painted, dilated upon its meaning, and then added: "It is a very old picture, conceived by a monk of Venice, the purport of which we believed as an article of faith, yea, even against the Christian faith."

When Martin had returned from Magdeburg to Mansfeld, the aged count Guenther was taken very sick and had old John Luther invited to his castle, where he remained and waited upon him till the count's death. When he returned home he spoke in high terms of praise to his family of the excellent testament of the count. In answer to the inquiry about the contents of this glorious last will and testament, he said that "he desired to depart from this world trusting alone in the bitter sufferings and death of our Lord Jesus Christ, consoling himself with His merits, and commending his soul to Him." "I thought," Luther afterwards said, "even as a young pupil, can this be such an excellent testament? For it seemed to me that if the count had bequeathed something considerable to churches or monasteries, this would have been a more

2*

note-worthy testament. But we see by this that our God has always, even in the midst of the darkness of the papacy, preserved many Christians unto eternal life, who have embraced the merits of His only Son and clung to them in faith. Therefore my father justly praised the count's last will as an excellent testament, although as a young pupil I did not then understand it."

CHAPTER IV.

LUTHER AT SCHOOL IN EISENACH.

After Luther had been but one year in Magdeburg, he went in 1498, by the command of his parents, to Eisenach, where his mother had many relatives. There he attended the Latin School connected with the church of St. George. Its rector was *John Trebonius*, a learned man and distinguished poet, who taught Grammar more skillfully than was the case elsewhere. Whenever he entered the school he took off his cap until he was seated upon his chair, from which he lectured. The other teachers were required to do the same, and when they occasionally forgot it, he admonished them earnestly. "For among these young pupils," he said, "sit those of whom God may make our future mayors, chancellors, learned doctors and rulers; although you do not know them now, it is proper that you should show them honor." In Dr. Luther this was abundantly realized.

In Eisenach his condition was, at first, exceedingly miserable. His relatives gave him no sufficient support. He was therefore compelled to seek his scanty subsistence by singing from house to house, and often to suffer hunger. At a later period he himself says: "Do not despise the boys who sing at the doors *panem propter Deum*, (i. e., bread for God's sake.) I too have been such a wanderer, going the rounds for bread, especially in my own dear town of Eisenach." He was so depressed on account of this destitution that he despaired of maintaining himself at school, and thought of returning home. But he was soon to experience how paternally God cared for him. Once he had been roughly repulsed from three different houses. The choir went on to the residence of Conrad Cotta, an honorable and wealthy citizen. Dame Ursula Cotta had long been "affectionately inclined toward the boy on account of his singing and of his fervent prayers at Church." She invited him in, gave him many presents, and a few days afterwards received him to her house and table. This kindness Luther never forgot. When Henry Cotta, her son, subsequently studied in Wittenberg, Luther received him to his table in turn. Of Ursula the report became current that God blessed her, after Martin's reception into her house, with unusual prosperity. May this stimulate us also to assist poor pupils in their studies.

In Martin a burning passion for learning was now aroused. He perceived "how beautiful a thing is knowledge," and studied Grammar, Rhetoric and Poetry with all industry. With his quickness of apprehension and fine talents he was soon in advance of his fellow pupils, and surpassed them in elocution and composition, both in verse and prose. There he laid the foundation of his future learning ; yea, the faithful instruction there received contributed to the fulfillment of the prophecy, which had lately been uttered concerning him in the monastery of the place.

About the year 1490 there lived in that monastery a Franciscan friar by the name of *John Hilten*, a quiet, pious old man. He had been thrown into a dungeon by the monks, because he had attacked several manifest abuses in monastic life. On account of age and the injurious influence of the prison, he became a prey to disease. He had the prior called, and notified him of his weakness. But when his superior, moved by pharisaic bitterness, and envy, encountered him with harsh expressions, he ceased to complain of his physical weakness, sighed deeply, and said, with earnest gesture, that he would bear such injustice cheerfully for Christ's sake, although he had written and taught nothing derogatory to the monastic order, but had attacked only gross abuses. Finally he said : "Another man shall appear in 1516, who shall extirpate you monks, and against whom ye shall be powerless." Concerning this Luther says in his Table Talk : "Now must John Huss be remembered, according to the prophecy of John Hilten, who was a monk at Eisenach, and who was slain within our own memory. He is reported to have said, when death was approaching : 'another shall come, whom ye shall see !' This prophecy was spoken when I was a boy and went to school at Eisenach."

Luther remained in the house of Cotta until his departure from Eisenach. There he also devoted his attention to Music, of which he was always fond, and learned to play the flute. Eisenach he always, in gratitude, called "his dear town," because he had "there learned and experienced so much good."

CHAPTER V.

LUTHER STUDIES AT ERFURT.

On the 17th of July, 1501, Luther, who had now attained the age of 18 years, went to the University of Erfurt. As he relates, this University was at that time "in such high repute that all others were in comparison looked upon as insignificant. How great was the pomp and glory when Masters were graduated, and torches were borne before them, and honors were showered upon them ; I hold that no other temporal joys equalled these. So was there also great splendor when the Doctor's degree was conferred; people rode about the city, dressed and decorated for the occasion. All has passed away now; but I wish that these ceremonies were still practiced."

There the celebrated *John of Wesel*, a witness of the truth, whose writings are still esteemed, had taught. Luther says of him: "John Weselia ruled the High School of Erfurt with his works, by the study of which I also was prepared for the Master's degree." Because he had attacked the corruption of the papacy, he was thrown into prison, where he died after two years of suffering, two years before Luther's birth. He foretold the Reformation in the words: "I perceive in the future that our souls shall faint with hunger, unless a star of mercy arise upon us from on high to dispel the darkness from our eyes, which the lies of the leaders have enchanted, and to restore the light, which shall, after so many years, finally break this yoke of Babylonish captivity.

His parents supported him from the proceeds of their mine, as he himself says in praise of his father. He "supported me, with great love and fidelity, at the high school of Erfurt, and by his arduous labor he aided in bringing me where I now am."

Among his teachers, *Jodocus Truttvetter* was one of the most esteemed, whom he calls the "first theologian and philosopher" and his "dear teacher and father." At a later period he reminded him, that from him he first learned the duty of receiving in faith the canonical Scriptures alone, while all others are subjected to criticism. From another of his teachers, *John Greffenstein*, a learned and pious man, he once heard that Huss had been condemned to death without conviction, and in violation of justice and law, by illiterate tyrants. Among others he also heard *Usingen*, who afterwards became his violent enemy, *John Bigard*, whom he subsequently recommended to a pastorate, "because he was a teacher whom he was under obligations to honor, and *Gerhard Hecker*, who accepted the Gospel and for this suffered manifold persecution.

At first Luther studied the subtle philosophy of his times, Logic and Dialectics, then Ethics and Physics. At the same time he read the best ancient Latin authors, such as Cicero, Virgil, Livy and Plautus. Nor did he, like the school-boys, read them for the sake of the words, but for their instructions, and as mirrors of human life. Therefore he paid close attention to the doctrines and proverbs of these writers, and as his memory was faithful, the most of that which he had read and heard was always at his command. Although he was naturally a sprightly and jovial youth, he still every morning commenced his studies with fervent prayer and attendance at Church, as it was his motto: "Diligence in prayer is the better half of study." He missed no lectures and was glad to ask his teachers questions, respectfully conversed with them, often reviewed lessons with his companions, and when there were no public lectures he was constantly to be found in the University library.

At one time, while he was examining the books one after another, that he might become acquainted with those that were good, he came upon the Latin Bible, which he had never before seen, though now in his twentieth year. He was astonished to find that it contained many more texts, Gospels and Epistles, than were usually explained in the postills and on the pulpits. Turning over the pages of the Old Testament, his eye caught the history of Samuel and his mother Hannah. This he read with avidity and with great delight; and because all this was new to him, he wished most heartily that God would, at some time, make him the possessor of such a book. Selnecker relates that when he read the words: "The Lord bringeth low and lifteth up; He raiseth up the poor out of the dust, and lifteth the beggar from the dunghill," he said: "How well adapted is this text for poor scholars, of whom I am one!" These words of Luther are also remarkable: "When I was a young man I heard learned men and good grammarians dispute with their opponents and say, that when we read the prophetic and apostolic writings we find a doctrine quite different from that which ye priests proclaim."

By his great industry he attained the first degree of academic honors as early as 1503, and thus secured the right to deliver philosophical lectures as a bachelor of arts. Not long afterwards he was taken very sick, so that he despaired of his life. But an old priest, who visited him, administered consolation, saying: "My dear bachelor, be of good comfort; you will not die of this illness. Our God will yet make a great man of you, who shall comfort many people. For upon him whom God loveth, and of whom he would make something blessed, he early imposes the holy cross, and in this school of affliction patient people learn much."

In that period, about 1593, another misfortune befell him. On Tuesday after Easter he was on his way home to visit his parents, with his arms at his side, as was the custom among students. Accidentally he struck his foot against his sword, when the blade fell out and sundered a main artery. He was about half a league from Erfurt, with but one companion. The blood flowed with alarming copiousness and could not be stanched; and when he laid himself upon his back, raising his leg and putting his finger upon the wound, his limb swelled frightfully. Finally a surgeon came from the city and dressed the wound. But Luther, when death seemed imminent, cried: "Mary, help me!" and in the night, when the wound again opened, so that he fainted, he again called only upon Mary. "At that time," he said in after years, "I should have died relying upon Mary."

In the early part of the year 1505, Luther attained the Master's degree. At his graduation he obtained the second position, and immediately commenced giving lectures upon Aristotelian Physics and Ethics. "Now there can be for me no cessation of study," said he, "if I am not to bring disgrace upon the German Masters." He left nearly the whole academic youth behind him, and his extraordinary gifts were now the admiration of the whole University. According to the will of his father, he was now to devote himself to the law, for which purpose he was supplied with books. For John Luther did not desire that he should become bishop, priest or monk, and be "supported by others in sumptuous living, instead of securing a livelihood by his own exertions." He rather thought that his son should, some day, be an honor to him by gaining temporal offices and dignities. He even thought of marrying him in wealth and honor; when suddenly Luther's course of life took a different direction.

The scholastic philosophy which Luther learned in Erfurt did not satisfy him. The thought constantly recurred: "O when wilt thou become holy and render satisfaction, that God may be gracious?" "The high schools," he says, "when they would render persons pious, set the judgment before them and render it as hot as possible. Thus they terrify the people and show them no way to escape from their terror." In Erfurt he twice repeated the vow to become holy and go upon a pilgrimage to Rome. Frequently he was so beset by such terrors, when he earnestly reflected upon the final judgment, that his life was endangered. Then one of his best friends, Alexius, was assassinated. And in the summer of 1505, when he was returning from a visit to his parents, he was overtaken, between Erfurt and the village of Stotterheim, by a violent thunder storm. The lightning struck at his feet and a terrific crash followed; he fell to the earth, and in his terror he cried : "dear Saint Anna, help, and I will immediately become a monk." He would enter a cloister to propitiate God with masses, and to merit salvation by monastic holiness. "I did not willingly become a monk," he said at a later period, "and least of all thought of pampering the stomach, but, encompassed with the sudden terror and anguish of death, I made a forced vow."

Luther now communicated his resolution to the monks. He afterwards said : "I intended to make my purpose known also to my parents, that I might hear their opinion upon it, as I was an only son, and heir to their property. But they taught me from Jerome that I should pay no regard to father and mother, but flee to the cross of Christ. They also adduced the words of our Lord : 'No man, having put his hand to the plough, and looking back, is fit for the kingdom of God.'"

Upon this he invited his friends to supper, delighted them once more with songs and instrumental music, and asked them to rejoice with him for the last time, as he was resolved to enter a monastery. They entreated him to change his purpose, but in vain. He said to them: "To-day ye see me, henceforth no more." He relates this himself, and adds: "Thus I remained firm in my resolution, thinking I would never leave the cloister." In the same night, the 17th of July, 1505, he hastened to the monastery of the Augustinians, and obtained admission, as previously agreed upon. He left all his possessions behind him, taking with him only Virgil and Plautus. The next morning he communicated the event to other friends by letter, and thanked them for all their manifestations of kindness. He also wrote to his parents, and sent them his ring of master of arts and his secular clothing.

His friends were saddened even to tears, that one so gifted should be buried alive in the cloister. Two whole days they, with other students, watched the monastery and besieged it, as it were, hoping to obtain Luther again: but in vain. The doors remained closed and bolted, and during a whole month no one was permitted to see him.

His father also was deeply grieved at the event. In his answer he addressed him in less respectful terms than formerly, and denied him all paternal favor. He even undertook the journey to Erfurt for the purpose of changing his son's mind; and when the latter excused himself on the ground of his being called by a terrible apparation from heaven, he replied: "God grant that it may not be a deception or a satanic illusion. Why, have you not heard that parents should be obeyed, and that nothing should be done without their knowledge and counsel?" But his father finally permitted himself to be persuaded by his friends. Two of his sons had died of the plague, and the information had been brought that Martin also was dead. Upon this his friends urged him that he should make the sacrifice and consent that his son should enter the "holy order." He had many scruples and was strongly disinclined, but said at last: "Let it pass; God grant that it may be well." Still he did not consent cheerfully.

According to monastic custom, Luther now dropped his baptismal name of Martin and assumed that of Augustine. This he subsequently looked upon with horror, and considered it a renunciation of his Baptism. Why God permitted him to enter the cloister he himself explains: "God, whose mercies are innumerable and whose wisdom is infinite, out of such error and sin brought forth great good. It seems to me that Satan foresaw in my youth what he now suffers. Therefore he so raged and raved against me and sought, with such manifold inventions, to hinder and destroy me, that I often marvelled, and wondered whether I was the only one among mankind that suffered his attacks. But it was God's will, as I now perceive, that I should learn, by my own experience, the philosophy of the schools and the holiness of the cloisters, that is, become acquainted with them by many sins and ungodly works, so that the ungodly people might not be able to boast against me, their future opponent, that I condemn what I do not understand."

With the wisdom of the papistic universities, Luther had already become acquainted. At a later period he justly called them schools of Satan. "For," he observes, "they have deserved nothing of me. I believe I do not lack understanding and my industry is known; but I have given my advice that young persons should avoid the philosophy and the theology of the schools as they would the death of their souls." Therefore he again repeats the apostolic warning: "Beware lest any man spoil you through philosophy and vain deceit," which he unhesitatingly applies to the philosophy of the schools. "What else have our universities in the whole world hitherto been than destroyers of excellent talents and corrupters of youth? Not only because these had full license to practice every sin and vice, which is the least ground for complaint; but because no sound, saving doctrine was taught, and the study of Christian doctrine was obscured by irksome, useless and mischievous sophistries, by which many good and noble minds were confused, and prevented from bearing valuable fruit." He complains of the "spectres of the high schools, which we have established with inhuman gifts, and by which we were burdened with many doctors, preachers, masters, priests and monks, that is, with great, rough, fat asses in red and brown caps, who taught us nothing good, but only rendered us more blind and frantic."

The papistic philosophy of the schools had driven Luther to despair. He entered the cloister for the purpose of finding salvation. We shall see whether he found it.

CHAPTER VII.

Luther's Monastic Labor.

When Luther had entered the monastery he asked for a Bible, and the monks gave him one. It was bound in red leather and fastened to a chain. He read it so eagerly that he knew the page and position of each passage. The whole day was sometimes spent in reflection upon an important sentence. He also committed many passages of the prophets to memory, although he did not then understand them.

But because he studied so much the monks became hostile to him, for they thought if the brother study he would gain dominion over them. In their monkish Latin they said to him: "Sacrum per nacrum et per civitatem," that is, "the sack on the back and off through the city;" and they frankly declared to him: "By begging, and not by studying, are the monasteries served and enriched." They imposed upon him the meanest and filthiest work; he was required to act as doorkeeper, to regulate the clock, to sweep the church, and even to clean the water closets. The most burdensome task to him, of course, was the incessant begging about the city. Luther obeyed without complaint. But the University of Erfurt, because he was a member of it, interceded for him with the prior, and Dr. *John von Staupitz*, the provincial of the Augustinians, also used his influence in his behalf, in consequence of which he was released from such servile work. It was Staupitz also who advised Luther above all things to study the Holy Scriptures, and to make himself intimately acquainted with them. This advice Luther followed with such assiduity that Staupitz was astonished at it, kept his eye particularly upon him, and stimulated him to continue his studies. But in those days there were few who entertained such thoughts; and Dr. Usingen, one of his monastic teachers, once said to him: "Why, brother Martin, what is the Bible? We should read the ancient teachers, who have drawn the substance of truth from the Bible. The Bible is the instigator of all disturbance."

Of his monastic brethren Luther says: "But few earnestly desired to be 'truly holy monks,' of whom I was one. The most of them were careless good fellows, accustomed to the easy life of the priesthood and the cloister, who never, during all their lives, experienced a true spiritual conflict." He now became acquainted with the holiness of the cloister in general. "Never," he says, "have I seen a fasting in the papacy that was truly such in the Christian sense ; to eat no meat they called fasting, while they ate the best fish with the most delicious condiments and drank good wine." "They taught that temporal possessions, vineyards and farms, should be despised, and yet were the greediest for them, and ate and drank the best that was to be had." "I saw a brother in the monastery who could eat five rolls, one of which was sufficient for me." Nothing was burdensome in the papacy ; everything was done willingly and cheerfully. Their fasting was easier for them than our eating. For each day of fasting there were three days of feasting. As an evening collation each monk received two pots of good beer and a mug of wine, with gingerbread or saltcake, so that drinking was rendered easy. The poor brethren thus looked like fiery angels, so very gaunt and pale were they!"— The monks are an idle, lazy people, answering to the description given by St. Peter, 2 Peter ii, 13, who look upon this life as given for pleasure. Nowhere is there more pride than in the cloisters, nowhere more insatiable avarice, lewdness, hatred and envy, which cannot be conquered, nor opposed, and by which they bite and rend each other. Their gluttony and drunkenness, indolence and disinclination to divine worship, are manifest. They are servants of their own bellies and swinish profligates."

"Still they lauded monasticism as the highest and most glorious state, and spoke of entering the cloister as of a new baptism. Accordingly, when Luther had taken the monastic vow the monks congratulated him that he "was now an innocent child that came forth pure from the baptismal font." All united in praising him for the "glorious deed" which he had performed, in virtue of which he "would be able to sanctify and save himself by his own works;" and he "heard with great delight such sweet praise and fine words concerning his own works;" for he at that time really believed that he could thus merit eternal life.

He himself tells us: "This monastic baptism they afterwards extolled still more highly, of which I shall mention an example. I was once in the Franciscan cloister at Arnstadt. At the table Dr. Henry Kuehne was present, whom they considered quite an extraordinary man. He lavished praises on the monastic order as a glorious thing, superior to all other conditions in life, because this new baptism gives it the singular advantage that, although he had regretted having become a monk and had thus rendered all his former good works and holy life worthless, he might repent, and form the resolution to become a monk if he were not one already, and this would be just as efficacious as his first entrance into the order, so that he would again be as pure as if he had just received baptism ; and this resolution he might repeat with the same effect as often as he chose. We young monks sat with mouths and noses open, and smacked our lips in devotion at the comfortable speech upon our holy monkery. The notion expressed was common among the monks."

At that time Luther also shared this opinion. Though others may have sought but carnal pleasure in the cloister, he led the most rigorous life in external holiness. In general, as a monk he was the most zealous papist to be found. He afterwards testified : "I can say of myself with truth that if, before the light of the Gospel had again dawned, there was one who sincerely revered the papistic ordinances and the traditions of the fathers, was zealous for them, deemed them sacred and considered their observance holiness, burned for them and defended them as necessary to salvation, I am that person." "I worshipped the pope, not for the sake of benefices and titles, but in singleness of heart, with an honest zeal, and for the glory of God." "Such saints as Paul himself, if not greater persecutors of Christ, were we, especially I, under the papacy. For so highly did I regard the pope's authority that I considered it a sin worthy of eternal death to deviate from him even in the smallest particular, and hence it was that I regarded Huss as such a damnable heretic that it seemed to me a sin even to think of him, and that I, to defend the pope's authority, would have been glad to light a fire for his destruction, and would have considered this an act of the highest obedience to God." "If any one had then taught what, by the grace of God, I now believe and teach, I would have torn him with my teeth."

How sincerely Luther then adored the pope is shown by the following story which he himself narrates. "Once, at Erfurt, in the library of the monastery, I, who was then a young theologian, found a book containing sermons of John Huss, and was impelled by an itching curiosity to see what the arch heretic had taught, as the book was left unburnt in the public library. In this I found so much that I was amazed, and wondered why a man who was so mighty in the Scriptures and so pious could have been condemned to the stake. But because his name was so horribly execrated that I then assumed that if any person would think well of it the walls would become black and the sun would cease to shine, I closed the book and went away with a wounded heart, but comforted myself with the thought that he might have written this before he became a heretic, as I was then not yet acquainted with the history of the Council of Constance."— "When I heard the name of Huss I was frightened, and did not venture to believe myself when I chanced upon a scriptural sermon from his pen." Thus terribly was Luther enchanted and captivated by the papacy. What a miracle of the Holy Spirit's grace was requisite to deliver him from it!

CHAPTER VIII.
Luther's Ordination as Priest.

The glory was great in the papacy when one was ordained as priest and read his first mass. "Blessed was the woman," says Luther, "who bare a priest, and father and mother, with all their friends, rejoiced." For "a consecrated priest was to other baptized Christians as the morning star to a smoking wick." Consecration raised the subject even above apostles, bishops and martyrs who had not been priests, "such great efficacy was in the chrism." "The first mass was held in high estimation and yielded much money, for offerings and gifts poured in like flakes in a snowstorm. Then the dear young lord had to dance with his mother, if she was living, so that the spectators wept for joy; if she was dead, he read mass for her soul and delivered her from purgatory."

The fathers had resolved that Luther's ordination should take place on Cantate Sunday, May 2, 1507. He invited his father and other friends to be present. The former made preparations as though he were going to a wedding, rode to the cloister in pomp, and presented his son twenty florins. Luther testifies: "When I read my first mass at Erfurt, I nearly died; for there was no faith, and I looked merely at my own worthiness, and was concerned merely not to be a sinner and to omit none of the manipulations and displays of the mass."

There was a regulation that, under pain of excommunication, no priest who had begun the mass and said the prayer should, without absolute necessity, leave the altar and permit another to finish the mass. To this penalty he came very near exposing himself.— When he had read the words: "I bring to Thee, the living God, this sacrifice," he fell into such consternation that he thought of leaving the altar, and would have done so if his preceptor had not deterred him. "For," he thought, "who am I that I should address the great Majesty, when all others tremble to appear in the presence of a prince or a king, or to address them?" "Since that time," he said to some friends, "I have always read mass with great horror."

When he was ordained the bishop placed the cup in his hand, and said: "Receive the power to sacrifice for the living and the dead." Of this Luther subsequently wrote: "That the earth did not then open and swallow us both up was owing to the infinite patience and long suffering of God." Notwithstanding all anti-Christian additions, however, he always acknowledged the validity of his ordination. Saying mass, on the other hand, he declared to be the greatest sin of his life, because he thus so frequently denied the only perfect sacrifice of Jesus Christ.

After the mass they gathered around the festive board. At the table the new priest began to converse with his father, whom he wished to convince of having been in the wrong, saying: "Dear father, why did you so vehemently oppose my becoming a monk, and grow angry at it, so that perhaps you are not even now quite satisfied with my choice, seeing it is such a comfortable, divine state." "Yes," said old John Luther, before all the doctors, masters and others, "Have you not thought of the 4th commandment, 'Honor thy father and thy mother?' In opposition to this commandment, you have forsaken me and your dear mother in our old age, and gone into the monastery against our will, when we should, because I have devoted so much expense and pains to your studies, have had some consolation and aid from you."— "But," answered Martin, "in this state I can be of more service to you, by prayer and other devotions, than if I had chosen some secular calling." "O, would to God," replied old Luther, "this were so." In general his aged father, even at this time, consented but reluctantly, and would rather have said: No, I am not pleased with it, which he indicated by saying: "I must be here and eat and drink, but would rather be away."

Luther afterwards declared: "At these words of my father, teaching me to remember the commandments, I was so terrified that it seemed as though a sword had pierced through my soul, and I could never forget them. Thus my father would not be satisfied with my spiritual calling as long as I was in the cloister. But afterwards when, enlightened by the grace of God, I laid aside the cowl and took a wife, he received me into his favor and I became his dear son again."

"Once, when he visited me, I again asked him why he had always opposed me in my monastic life. 'O, it always seemed to me,' he said, 'that there was nothing in the clerical order but dissimulation and knavery.' Thus my father became reconciled again, from which it is manifest that God always preserved many honest hearts even under the papacy."

When Luther had become a priest, his brother monks took the Bible away from him again and gave him the writings of the schoolmen. To render obedience, he read them so diligently that he could repeat several almost word for word from memory. But chiefly did he study the works of Augustine, which he also retained most readily. As often, however, as he found time and opportunity, he hid himself in the library of the monastery and faithfully pondered his dear Bible.

CHAPTER IX.
LUTHER'S CONFLICTS IN THE CLOISTER.

Luther sought to merit the grace of God by his own works; therefore his experience in the cloister was "heartily and murderously bitter." Day and night he tortured and tormented himself with fasting and prayer, with singing and study, with lying on beds of pain, with cold and weeping: he designed to take heaven by storm. Sometimes he read and wrote so zealously that he forgot the *horas canonicas*—the prayers prescribed for certain hours. To satisfy his conscience and the papal ordinances, he would then lock himself in a cell and, without eating or drinking, make up what had been neglected. In this way he so fretted his mind that once he could not sleep for five weeks and was near mental derangement. Nay, it was not enough for him most punctually to observe the rules of his order; he imposed upon himself additional tasks. Thus he could say of himself with truth: "It is certain that I was a pious monk, and so scrupulously observed the regulations that I can say, if ever a monk entered heaven by monkery I shall enter also. All my companions in the cloister who knew me, will testify to this. For if these things had continued I would have tortured myself to death with watching, praying, reading and other labors."

But all his good works brought him no consolation; he was always sad and sorrowful.

Therefore he redoubled his zeal and employed all the means which the Romish Church offered and recommended to obtain peace. "We did everything," he says, "that was suggested to us in the name of the Church, in order that we might find comfort and assistance, and not despair of divine grace; but instead of consoling us they led us to the devil and plunged us still more deeply into anxiety and terror; for there was nothing that could give us assurance, as they must themselves confess their doctrine to be, that a person cannot and should not be certain that he is under divine grace."

"I had chosen," he relates, "twenty-one saints, read mass every day, and each time called upon three of them, so that I completed the round in a week; and especially did I invoke the holy virgin, whose woman's heart I thought more easily moved to propitiate the Son. The petitions and ejaculations of all, including the holy monks, were of this import: 'Dear mother of God, assist us, and intercede for us against the rigorous judgment of thy Son, else there is for our souls no comfort, nor help, nor counsel.' But with all my masses, prayers, watchings, chastity, I could never succeed in getting so far that I could say: Now I am certain that God is gracious to me, or: now I have experienced that my order and strict life has helped me and conducts me to heaven."

In his anxiety he went to confession daily and thus wearied his confessors. The papists teach that whoever would receive forgiveness of sin must, in auricular confession, specify all his sins. But this is impossible, and hence Luther never knew whether he had confessed all. Confession, therefore, was to him a rack. Nor did the absolution comfort him ; for it was imparted to him with the condition that he must himself atone for his sin by penitence and good works. But he did not know how much was requisite for such satisfaction. His confessors, indeed, imposed upon him certain penances, which he most conscientiously performed ; but he still could not know whether God was really gracious to him on this account. His confessors pointed him to purgatory as a hope for the supply of any deficiencies in his penance. But neither did this quiet him ; for no mortal could tell how long the expiation in purgatory must endure. Some were of the opinion that there could be no deliverance from it, because seven years penance was requisite for each mortal sin. Indulgences and masses for souls should, indeed, render them assistance ; but this, too, was a very uncertain consolation, because no one could tell how many masses are necessary to redeem a soul from purgatory. "O, it is a terrible plague in Christendom," Luther exclaims, "that people are led into uncertainty and left to trust in their uncertain works."

The torment of soul which he suffered under this false papistic doctrine, he thus describes : "When I became a monk I gave all possible diligence to live uprightly according to the rules, was accustomed often to repent of my sins in sincerity and to confess all as far as possible, and performed the penances laid upon me as strictly as I could. And yet my conscience could never find rest and assurance, but always remained in doubt, since I thought : in this and this thou hast sinned, here thou hast not sufficiently repented of thy sins, and there something was forgotten in thy confession. Therefore the more I sought to support my doubting, weak and troubled conscience by human ordinances, the more its doubts, and weakness, and trouble increased from day to day; and the more I sought thus to observe the human ordinances, the more I transgressed them. In short, the more sedulously I endeavored to become holy through my order, the worse I became. For St. Paul declares it to be impossible for man to obtain peace of conscience by the works of the law ; much more is it impossible to obtain it by human ordinances, without the promise and Gospel of Christ."

Nor did the reception of the Lord's Supper afford him any comfort. This sweet and solacing sacrament also had the papists corrupted with false doctrine, and thus they had deprived Christians of all the joy which it was designed to give. "For they had taught us," he says, "that we must attain a purity in which we are free from every particle of daily sin, and a dazzling holiness, upon which God can scarcely bear to look. This I could not find in myself, and therefore the sacrament filled me with terror." "When I was most devout I went to the altar with doubts, and with doubts I again departed. If I said my penitential prayers I doubted; if I neglected to say them I despaired: for we all held the delusion that we could not pray, and would not be heard, unless we were as pure and sinless as the saints in heaven."

From this we perceive how the Romish doctrine brought Luther to the most horrible despair. By its influence he had lost Christ, who was no more regarded as his dear Savior, but whom he was taught rather to consider an angry, terrible Judge, as they pictured him sitting upon the rainbow. He sought to propitiate God by his good works, but just because he was honest and sincere he saw this to be impossible. He followed the papistic doctrine most faithfully until he learned by experience that it is false and comfortless—a well without water. Accordingly he thus describes his condition in the cloister: "The executioner and the devil were in our hearts, and fear, trembling, terror and anxiety tormented us day and night. In fine, a cloister is a hell, in which the devil is abbot and prior, and monks and nuns are the lost souls."

Amid these conflicts Luther must have perished had not God, through His saints, of whom there were some hidden even in the papacy, mercifully comforted him.

CHAPTER X.

How Luther was Consoled in the Cloister.

God comforted Luther's bruised heart especially through Dr. Staupitz. To him Luther often confessed, and complained of his trials. Staupitz replied: "I have never experienced such conflicts; but as far as I can see and understand, they are more necessary for you than eating or drinking." If he went to another, he received no better answer; no confessor knew anything about them. Then he thought that no one had any such trials but himself, and became as pale as death.— Finally Staupitz said to him at the table, where he was so sad and dejected: "Why are you so sorrowful, brother Martin?" Luther replied: "Ah, whither shall I go?" Staupitz said: "O, you know not how salutary and necessary such trials are for you; without them nothing good would become of you.— God does not send them to you in vain. You shall see that God purposed to use you for the accomplishment of great things." "This," Luther says, "I accepted as words of comfort and as the voice of the Holy Ghost."

Once he said to Staupitz: "Why, my dear Doctor, God deals so terribly with men; who can serve Him when He lays about Him thus?" Staupitz answered: "Dear Sir, learn to think differently of God; if He dealt otherwise, how could He subdue stubborn heads? He must restrain the lofty trees that they grow not into the heavens. God strikes to heal, that we, who would otherwise be oppressed, may be delivered and redeemed."

He also frequently wrote to Staupitz, and once in a letter uttered the complaint: "O my sin, sin, sin!" Staupitz made this reply: "You would be without sin, and yet have no sin in reality. Christ is the forgiveness of real sins, such as the murder of parents, open blasphemy, contempt of God, adultery, &c. These are sins in truth. You must keep a record of real sins, if Christ is to help you, and not be engaged in such mummery and puppetry, making every trifle a sin."

At another time, when Luther had fallen into great temptations, Staupitz comforted him with power, saying: "Why, would you be only a feigned sinner and have only a feigned Savior? Accustom yourself to think of Jesus as a real Savior, and of yourself as an actual sinner. God is not engaged in vain show or idle jest when he sends His Son into the world to die for us."

"When I was a young man," Luther relates, "as I was walking in the procession in priestly robes at Erfurt, on Corpus Christi day, I was so terrified at the Sacrament, which Dr. Staupitz carried, that I was all in a perspiration, and thought I must die of fear. After the procession I told Dr. Staupitz of my anguish. He said: 'Your thoughts are not Christ; for Christ does not terrify; He only consoles.' These words I received joyfully, and they gave me great consolation."

When Luther was once cruelly tortured by the doubt whether he was predestined to eternal life, and told Staupitz of his distress, the latter comforted him with the words: "Predestination is understood and found in the wounds of Christ and nowhere else. For it is written, 'Hear ye Him.' The Father is too highly exalted, therefore He says: 'I will give you a way by which you may come to me, namely Christ: believe in Him and cling to Him, and ye shall in due time know who I am.' For God is incomprehensible, and we cannot understand and fathom what He is, much less what his purposes are; we cannot know Him, nor will He be apprehended without Christ. If you would dispute about predestination, begin at the wounds of Christ, and all doubtful disputations will at once cease. Therefore cling to the word, in which God has revealed Himself, and adhere to it steadfastly; in this you have the true way of life and salvation, if you only believe it. But when we would follow our own thoughts and reason we forget God; then the *laudate* (praise) ceases and the *blasphemate* (blasphemy) begins, as in Christ all treasures are contained, and without him none are accessible. Therefore impress Christ on your heart, and predestination is accomplished and you possess it. For God has ordained that His Sons hould suffer, not for the just, but for sinners. Whoever believes this, is his dear child. Hence, as regards this article, we should think thus : God is true, and does not lie nor err ; this I know; he has bestowed upon me his only begotten Son with all his gifts, has granted me Holy Baptism, the sacrament of the true body and blood of His Son, with all manner of gifts, both temporal and eternal. When I thus reflect upon the great and unspeakable benefits which God our heavenly Father, in pure grace and mercy, has, for Christ's sake, conferred upon me, without any merit, good works or worthiness of mine, as His word testifies, and adhere to this, predestinanion is sweet and consoling, and remains sure and steadfast, especially as I know that God Himself speaks to me in His word and through His servants."

Once when the subject of conversation was repentance, Staupitz said : "Only that is true repentance which flows from love to God and His righteousness." These words penetrated into Luther's soul like the sharp arrow of the mighty. He searched the Scriptures more fully, and experienced the sweet joy of finding that all the passages of Scripture harmonized with the proposition. Afterwards nothing had a more pleasing sound than the word repentance, which before was the most bitter.

There were also several others who comforted him in his trials. Thus his confessor once said to him, when he had confessed his sins : "You are a simpleton ; God is not angry with you, but you are angry with Him."

Luther subsequently called these "precious, great and glorious words, which were spoken before this Gospel light had dawned."

At one time he complained with tears to his teacher of his conflicts, when he received the reply: "What are you doing, my son? Do you not know that our Lord Himself has commanded us to hope and believe?" Luther says: "This one word 'commanded' afforded me the consolation afterwards to know that we should and must believe the absolution and forgiveness of sin, which I had often heard before, but which, in my foolish thoughts, I had supposed did not concern me and were not to be believed by me, hearing them as vain words."

Especially did Luther frequently mention with esteem and gratitude an old monastic brother, who referred him to the words in the Apostles' Creed: "I believe in the remission of sins." This article he thus explained: "It is not enough for you to believe in general that God forgives sins, but you must believe that He forgives you, you, you. For we are saved by grace through faith." By these words Luther was not only strengthened, but his attention was also directed to the truth that we are justified through faith. Upon this he read many commentaries, but by frequent conversations with the old brother and by the consolation which he experienced he soon perceived what sorry helps were the commentaries then in vogue. He therefore read and compared, with daily prayer, the declarations and example of the prophets and apostles upon the subject, and thus the light became gradually brighter in his soul. In the writings of Augustine, also, he found many clear sentences which confirmed him in this doctrine concerning faith and in the consolation which it brought to his heart.

CHAPTER XI.
Luther is called to Wittenberg.

In the year 1502 the Elector Frederick of Saxony had, through Dr. Martin Mellerstadt and Dr. John Staupitz, established the university of Wittenberg. Staupitz desired to elevate the study of theology in the new university ; and because he had observed in brother Martin great talents and earnest piety, he brought him, in the year 1508, to the convent at Wittenberg. His departure from Erfurt took place in such haste that scarcely his nearest friends were aware of it.

In Wittenberg he was at first required to teach the Dialectics and Physics of Aristotle. But the chair of philosophy was distasteful to him, and he would therefore from the beginning, as he wrote to his friend John Braun, gladly have exchanged it for that of theology, especially of the theology which searches for "the kernel of the nut, the heart of the wheat, and the marrow of the bones. But," he adds,

"God is good, and man often, nay, always, errs in his judgment. He is our God; may He Himself lead us according to His kindness eternally."

On the 9th of March, 1509, in his 26th year, Luther became bachelor of theology with the designation *"ad biblia,"* i. e., for the interpretation of the Bible. He now devoted himself entirely to the study of the Scriptures, and began to dispute against the principles of the sophists, which were then everywhere in vogue, and to inquire into the true and certain ground of our salvation. Therefore he based his lectures exclusively upon the Holy Scriptures, and considered these more exalted, more thorough, and more certain than all sophistry and scholastic theology. By this course he attracted so much attention that even then already intelligent men were astonished at it. The celebrated Mellerstadt, who was then rector of the university, often said of him: "This monk will confound all the doctors, introduce a new doctrine, and reform the Romish Church; for he devotes himself to the writings of the prophets and apostles, and takes his position uqon the word of Jesus Christ, which no one is able to refute or overthrow with philosophy or sophistry, with the weapons of the Albertists or Thomists, or with all the Tartaretus."

Staupitz also strongly urged Luther to engage in preaching. But as it seemed to the latter no slight matter to speak in God's stead to the people, he was not easily persuaded. He found fifteen pretexts for declining the call to preach. At last he said: "Doctor, you will deprive me of my life; I shall not hold out three months." To this Staupitz replied: "Well, in God's name be it so; what then? Our Lord has great works in hand and needs men of wisdom on high also." He was thus compelled to yield, and to preach to the brethren in the hall of the convent, afterwards publicly to the congregation.

The little church in which Luther at first preached, Myconius thus describes: "In the new Augustine convent at Wittenberg, the foundation of a Church had been laid, but had been brought no further than to a level with the ground. In the middle of the square an old wooden chapel, thirty feet long and twenty wide, was standing yet, which was daubed with clay, very much dilapidated, and propped up on all sides. It had an old sooty little gallery, upon which twenty persons could stand in an emergency. At the wall towards the South was an old pulpit of rough boards, elevated about three feet above the floor. In short, it looked in all respects like the stable at Bethlehem in which Christ was born, as this is usually represented by the painters. In this poor and wretched chapel it pleased God that His holy Gospel and the dear child Jesus should be born anew, and that all the world should see how sweet and lovely they are, and what comfort and salvation they bestow. There were thousands of cathedrals and splendid churches, but God did not choose them for the purpose. But his chapel soon became too small and Luther was ordered to preach in the parish church : thus the child Jesus was brought into the temple."

A ray of light had then already penetrated the soul of Luther, which groped in the darkness of the papacy. God had led him to the Holy Scriptures and he chose them as his loadstar ; he felt that they alone could give him the truth and peace which he sought. But they were yet a sealed book to him, and therefore he still clung to Rome. According to the purpose of God, however, the Sun of Righteousness should again rise in his view, and through him shine upon the nations who languished in the papistic shadow of death. The way in which God led him to the knowledge of the truth was wonderful. Luther had taken up the epistle to the Romans to explain it.— When he came to the passage from the prophet Habakkuk : "The just shall live by faith," this sentence, by the power of God, made such a deep impression upon his mind that, whatever he was engaged in, he thought he heard the words : "The just shall live by faith." He was conscious that his soul was deeply moved, but he knew not how to still the commotion.

At the same time God in His wisdom so directed him that he, by his own observation, became acquainted with the seat of the papacy.

CHAPTER XII.

Luther's Pilgrimage to Rome.

In 1510 Luther was sent, on business pertaining to the convent, in company with a monastic brother, to Rome. He was the more willing to undertake the journey as he hoped, by a visit to the holy places, as they were called, to find rest and comfort for his conscience. But the further he proceeded on his way, the more frequently and the more vehemently he thought the words were sung in his ears: "The just shall live by faith."

Before Luther had reached the Appenines he chanced to meet several monks who ate meat on Friday. He admonished them, in kind and courteous words, entreating them to remember that the pope had forbidden the eating of meat. The monks were not a little alarmed at these words, fearing that, if the matter should become known, they would incur danger and public disgrace. Therefore they agreed to put Luther out of the way. But God so ordered it that the porter notified him of this bloody intent, and he accordingly made good his escape in the best way that he could. At another time, when he and his companion had slept the whole night with the windows open, they were so affected by the unhealthy night-air that they could proceed only a mile on the following day. Their great thirst placed them in constant temptation to drink water, which in that region is fatal. Finally they revived and refreshed themselves with two pomegranates, by which God preserved their lives.

Of his journey he relates: "In Lombardy on the Po, there is a very wealthy cloister of the Benedictine order, which has an annual income of 36.000 ducats. There such luxury and voluptuousness prevails that 12.000 ducats are appropriated to banquets, 12.000 to the buildings, and the remaining third to the convent and the brethren. I was in the cloister and was treated sumptuously."

When Luther first perceived the city of Rome he fell upon his knees, lifted up his hands and exclaimed: "Holy Rome, I salute thee! thrice holy because of the blood of the martyrs which flowed in thee." There he sought in deep devotion to satisfy his soul.— "In Rome," he relates, "I also was a crazy saint, ran through every church and grot, and believed every lie that left its stench in the city. I embraced the opportunity also of reading masses there, and was then very sorry that my father and mother were living yet, as I would have been glad to redeem them from Purgatory by masses and other precious works and prayers." But even when he read mass with the most devout feeling, he experienced in his heart all the more sensibly the power of the words: "The just shall live by faith." There was at the Church of St Peter's a flight of stairs called Pilate's Staircase, which the papists represented as having been transported thither from the judgment hall in

Jerusalem. The pope had promised plenary indulgence to those who should ascend these stairs on their knees. Luther undertook this work with the purpose of propitiating God, whom he thought highly offended, and of expiating his sins, looking upon this as the best and the last means to find comfort. But whilst he crept up the stairs he felt as though a voice of thunder cried to him in terrible tones: "The just shall live by faith." This deprived him, indeed, of all the comfort which he had expected to obtain there by his own works and efforts, but rendered him all the more attentive to the power of the words, which should be the means of showing him the true way to heaven.

Rome was lauded at that time as the "fountain of righteousness;" but Luther learned to know it differently. He relates: "I was at Rome, though not long,—read many masses there, and also saw others engaged in them, so that I tremble when I think of it. There, among other vile, coarse buffooneries I heard courtesans boast at the table, and making merry over the circumstance, that some in saying mass had used the words: *Panis es, panis manebis, vinum es, vinum manebis*, that is: bread thou art and bread thou shalt remain, wine thou art and wine thou shalt remain, and that they had thus elevated the host. I was a young monk who was truly sincere and pious, and such things pained me. What should I think? What other thoughts than these should occur to me : Is it possible that here in Rome such mockery is indulged in openly at the table ? how if all of them, the pope, cardinals, courtesans and all, say mass thus? How nicely then would I have been deceived, who heard them say so many masses. I was quite disgusted too at the hustling levity with which, helter skelter, they performed the mass, as if it were a puppet-show ; for before I had reached the Gospel the priest at my side had finished his mass and cried to me: *Fratello, passa, passa,* quick, quick, send her son home to our Lady speedily.' "

He also learned in Rome how shamefully believers were there deceived with spurious relics. He testifies : "This I can say confidently, from what I saw and heard at Rome, that it is not known in that city where the remains of St. Paul or St. Peter lie, or whether they lie there at all. The pope and the cardinals are well aware that they do not know it. Yet on the day of St. Peter and Paul they set up two heads, pretend that they are the real heads of these apostles, and lead the common people to believe it, who crowd around them in devout wonder ; but the pope and the cardinals, with their attendants, know right well that they are two wooden heads, carved and painted. Thus they deceive also with their veronicas, pretending that our Lord's face is impressed upon the handkerchief, while it is nothing but a little, square, black board, with a veil hanging over it, before which hangs a curtain that is drawn when the Veronica is shown, so that the people see nothing more than a screen before a black board, and this they call showing and seeing the Veronica, with which shameless lie great indulgences are offered and great devotion is displayed."

In Italy Luther found priests of the grossest ignorance. To the question : how many sacraments are there? they answered : three, the sprinkling brush, the censer and the cross. He says of them : "The greater their honors and dignities, the more wantonly they sin, so that it has long since become a proverb : the nearer Rome, the worse Christian." In general he is unable to find words to describe the horrible abominations which he saw in Rome. "Not the least tittle of divine order is observed at Rome, nay, its observance is ridiculed as folly. All evil examples of spiritual and secular knavery flow into the world from Rome as from a sea of wickedness. No one believes what villany and what horrible sins and vices are practiced there ; to be convinced of it a person must see and hear and experience it for himself."

"At Rome, passing down a wide street which leads to St. Peter's, I saw a stone statue representing a pope under the figure of a woman, holding a sceptre, clothed in the papal mantle, and bearing a child in her arms. No pope passes through this street, as he must not behold this statue. It is a young woman of Mayence, who was brought by a cardinal to

England in the character of a boy, and finally conducted to Rome. There she was elected pope by the cardinals, but her shame was exposed, as she was publicly delivered of a child in that street.

"I must here relate an occurrence showing what opinions we should form of the holy scoundrels and murderers of the Romish see. At Rome I was told the following : 'About seven German miles this side of the city there is a village called Roncilion. In the time of Paul I. there was an official of the pope in that place who saw the scandalous, satanic proceedings of the pope and his parasites at Rome, and withheld from him the annual dues from his office. The pope summoned him, but he refused to appear. All the commands of the pope he despised. At length the pope excommunicated him, but he remained indifferent. Then the pope had the bells tolled, and, with the pulpit lights extinguished, had him anathematized according to custom, but he concerned himself nothing about it. Finally, because such obstinate disobedience of the pope passes for heresy according to Romish law, he had the official's picture painted on paper, with many devils about his head and on either side, and had this brought before the court, accused, and condemned to the stake as a heretic, and instantly the paper was hurried to the fire and burned. The official then also had the pope painted in the midst of his cardinals, all full of devils over head and round about, convened a court, and had the pope and cardinals charged with being the vilest knaves on earth, who did incalculable injury to the poor people, who, when their chief dies, place at their head the wickedest person to be found among them, and who are well worthy of hell-fire ; and many witnesses were brought to prove this ; upon which the judge, the official and the plaintiffs cried that they should be burned, and instantly, in the name of a thousand devils, they hurried the pope and cardinals away to the fire ; till at last the pope silenced him by force.' This story may be laughable, but it shows a terrible evil, how the pope causes great scandal by his horrible, devilish wickedness at Rome, and how the people who see it are offended and become epicurean like themselves. For nearly all who return from Rome bring a papistic conscience with them, that is an epicurean faith, as it is certain that the pope and cardinals with their whole gang of rogues believe nothing, and only laugh when they hear faith mentioned. I myself heard it said publicly on the streets in Rome, that if there is a hell Rome is built over it, that is, next to the devils themselves there is not a more depraved crew than the pope and his toadies.''

Thus Luther was called to become himself thoroughly acquainted with Rome, in order that, in due time, he might be the better qualified to bear testimony against it. Therefore he says himself : ''I would not for a thousand florins have missed seeing Rome, for then I would always fear that I might do injustice to the pope ; but we speak that which we have seen."

When he had accomplished his mission in Rome he returned home poor and dejected. He had been undeceived. He had expected to find holiness and consolation in Rome, and he found diabolical wickedness instead. In Bologne he was attacked by such a severe pain in his head and ringing in his ears that he thought his end was approaching, and he fell into a profound melancholy. Then suddenly the words again presented themselves to his soul : "The just shall live by faith," but now with a radiance which they had not before. He was revived and wonderfully refreshed as if by a ray of heavenly light. Never before, frequently and zealously as he had studied the epistle to the Romans, had he so clearly and forcibly understood the meaning of these words. Now it was written in his soul, with divine clearness and firmness, that the righteousness so often mentioned by the apostle is the righteousness of Christ, which God graciously imputes to faith. When he had returned to Wittenberg he examined further into the matter with unremitting diligence, and had the unutterable joy to find this truth everywhere confirmed. "Then," he writes, "the whole Scriptures were opened to me, and also heaven itself. Immediately I felt as if born anew, as if I had found the open gate of paradise. Henceforward, also, I saw the beloved Holy Scriptures with other eyes. Therefore I compared all the passages I could remember, and found it to be all the more certain that the righteousness of God signifies the righteousness which He gives us, because this accords with the scriptural mode of speaking, e. g., the work of God means the work which He performs in us, the power of God means the power which he gives us, the wisdom of God means the wisdom which he bestows upon us, and so with God's strength, God's salvation, God's glory, &c. As I had previously with all my heart detested the words, 'righteousness of God,' I now began to value and love them as the sweetest and most consoling words in the Bible. In very truth this passage of St. Paul was now to me the very gate of paradise."

CHAPTER XIII.

LUTHER BECOMES DOCTOR OF THE HOLY SCRIPTURES.

In the year 1512 Staupitz, Luther s superior, and the whole cloister, resolved that brother Martin should be created Doctor of the Holy Scriptures, and this resolution was communicated to him under a tree in the cloister at Wittenberg. But when Luther excused himself on the ground that he was a feeble and sickly brother who had not long to live, and begged that one better qualified and with better health might be selected, Staupitz answered jestingly : "It seems that our God will soon have much to do in heaven and upon earth, therefore He will need many industrious doctors to perform the work. Whether you live or die God will need you in His council.— Therefore accept what your convent imposes, as you are bound by your profession to obey it and me. As regards the expenses, our gracious Elector, Duke Frederick, will defray them from his treasury for the benefit of this university and cloister." This was also done, as the Elector had heard Luther preach and had admired his spirit, the energy of his speech, and the useful doctrines which he proclaimed.

Accordingly on the 18th of October, 1512, at one o'clock in the afternoon, Luther was, in the presence of many members of the University and other reverend gentlemen, declared a licentiate of Sacred Theology by Dr. Andrew Bodenstein *Carlstadt*, at that time Dean and Archdeacon of the Church of All Saints. On the following day, after the fathers and guests, summoned by the great bell, had assembled as before, he was honored by Dr Carlstadt with the title of Doctor of Sacred Theology. By this regular and public vocation and by the solemn oath which he had made to God, the Holy Scriptures, and the University at Wittenberg, Luther often consoled himself in his great troubles and conflicts, when Satan and the world would seek to terrify him with the question who had ordered him to do this, and how he would answer for making such a disturbance in all Christendom. He could joyously testify: "I, Doctor Martin Luther, was called and forced to become a doctor from mere obedience, without any choice of mine. I was constrained to accept the doctorate and to swear allegiance to my beloved Holy Scriptures, and to vow that I would preach them faithfully and purely. While doing this, Popery obstructed my path and desired to stop me; but you see what has happened to it, and worse still will befall it; it shall not hinder me."

As in the same year the council called him to be preacher, he studied the Scriptures more zealously and more earnestly than ever. In order to understand them more thoroughly he diligently studied the Hebrew language, in which the Old Testament was originally written, and the Greek, which is the original language of the New Testament. In his lectures he explained the Epistle to the Romans and the Psalms so clearly and attractively, that all pious and intelligent Christians could not otherwise than believe a beautiful and lovely light to have risen upon them after the gloom of the long night; for he pointed out the difference between the Law and the Gospel, and refuted the terrible error, which was then taught in all the schools and churches, as it had been taught in our Lord's time by all the scribes and pharisees, that man is able to merit forgiveness of sins by his own good works and to become just before God by external piety and social integrity. He again directed the hearts of men to the Son of God, pointed, like John the Baptist, to the Lamb of God who has fully discharged all our obligations and taken away our sins, and taught that our sins are forgiven for Christ's sake alone, without any merit of ours, which blessing is to be appropriated by a living faith and retained until death. At the same time he also wrote many consolatory and instructive letters to troubled consciences, among which is the following to George Spenlein, a beloved brother in the cloister of Memmingen:

"I should like to know the state of your soul. Is it not at last tired of its own righteousness and desirous to refresh itself in the righteousness of Christ and to trust in that? In our days many are attacked by presumptuous madness, and especially those who labor with all their might to become righteous.— They do not understand the righteousness of God which is given to us abundantly and freely in Christ, and seek in their own power to do good, until they can have joyfulness to appear before God as persons who are adorned with good works and merits, which is impossible. When you were with us you entertained this opinion, or rather error, and so did I, and I am yet struggling against it and have not entirely overcome it. Therefore, my dear brother, learn to know Christ and Him crucified; learn to sing praises to Him and, despairing of yourself, to say: Thou my Lord Jesus, art my righteousness, and I am Thy sin. Thou hast assumed what was mine and given me what was Thine."

Thus the glorious light of the Gospel arose again through Martin Luther; for he showed from the word of God what man must do to be saved, and treated especially of repentance, of forgiveness of sin, of faith, and of the true consolation of the cross. All pious hearts were moved by the sweetness of this doctrine, and the learned were glad that Christ and the prophets and apostles were led forth, as it were, from the darkness and dust in which they had lain. At the same time Luther contended against the Aristotelian philosophy, by the aid of which the papists sought to support their doctrines, and proved that the Christian faith, and how to lead a Christian life and die a happy death, must be learned from the Scriptures, and not from the heathen Aristotle. Besides this he led a godly, blameless life. His conversation corresponded with his teaching, so that his sincerity was manifest. Neither did he make rash changes in the existing Church usages, but was rather a rigid preserver of order. By these means he gained the affections of his hearers and a high reputation.

The beautiful sciences and liberal arts had at that time received a new impulse through John Reuchlin and Erasmus. Whilst Luther gradually obtained clearer perceptions of the truth, his friends, Staupitz, Spalatin and others, sought to advance these sciences in Wittenberg and advocated their claims before the Elector. They soon flourished there in their beauty, and the ancient languages especially were studied diligently, which, conjoined with fervent prayer, the holy cross, and earnest meditation, are the best interpreters of the divine word. And because a better method of instruction was introduced by Luther, many clear and gifted minds became disgusted with the barbarous and scholastic doctrine of the monks and directed their attention to the Gospel. Thus Luther was enabled, on the 17th of May, 1517, to report to John Lange : "Our theology and St. Augustine, by the help of God, prosper and prevail in our university. Aristotle is gradually descending from his throne and will soon fall, perhaps forever.— The lectures on the Sententiaries have fallen into great contempt, and no one can expect hearers unless he lecture upon this theology, that is upon the Bible, St. Augustine, or some other true Church father."

In 1516 the plague prevailed in Wittenberg and John Lange had advised Luther to flee. He answered, "Whither shall I go? I hope the world will not crumble to ruin if brother Martin leave it. When the pestilence increases I will scatter the brethren in all directions, but I am placed here and dare not flee. I do not say this because I have no fear of death, for I am not the apostle Paul, but only his interpreter; nevertheless I hope that God will deliver me from all my fears."

In 1517 Luther was in Dresden and on the 25th of July preached before the duke. In this sermon he said that no one is permitted to cast away the hope of salvation, inasmuch as those who attentively hear the word of God are the true disciples of Christ and are elected and appointed to eternal life. He dwelt upon this point and showed that the doctrine of election, if it have its starting point in Christ, has a peculiar power to expel the fear which drives the soul, in the feeling of its unworthiness, away from God, in whom it should seek refuge. At table the duke asked the governess, Barbara of Sala, how she liked the sermon, and he received the answer: "If I could hear another such sermon I could die in far greater peace." This offended the duke who said, in his papistic blindness, that he would give a great deal if he had not heard such a sermon, the tendency of which is to render people presumptuous. The desire of Barbara, however, was fulfilled, for in the course of a month she was taken ill and joyfully departed from this world. Luther never visited Dresden afterwards.

Commissioned by Staupitz, Luther in 1516 and 1517 visited forty Augustine cloisters in Misnia and Thuringia. He performed the difficult task with great fidelity, establishing schools and admonishing the monks diligently to read the Bible and to lead a holy, peacable and sober life. This visitation afforded him opportunities to become still better acquainted with the corruption prevalent in the cloisters, and God thus continued to prepare him for the great work of the Reformation.

CHAPTER XIV.
Tetzel's Scandalous Indulgence Traffic.

At this time the occupant of the papal throne was Leo X., an ungodly man, who was given to all vice and licentiousness and who believed nothing. By his debauchery and intemperance he had become well-nigh blind. When cardinal Bembo once referred him to the Holy Scriptures on some point, he uttered the shocking words: "Ah, what money has the fable about Christ ever brought us?" Luther relates of him: "When he wished to amuse himself and provoke merriment for pastime, he would call two clowns, who disputed before his table on the immortality of the soul, the one affirming, the other denying it.— When, at the close of the debate, they both appealed to the pope's decision, the most holy father, by his holy Romish spirit, gave this judgment, addressing the advocate of the affirmative: Although you have adduced good reasons, I shall concur with him who holds that we die like other brutes; for your view produces melancholy and sadness, while the other generates gayety and good spirits."

But to carry out his revelry and lasciviousness the pope needed a great deal of money. To obtain this he proclaimed, ostensibly for the purpose of continuing the work upon the splendid Church of St. Peter, a general indulgence, and commissioned the Elector Albert of Mayence, who was also Archbishop, to have this indulgence preached in Germany. Albert chose for this work the Dominican monk *John Tetzel*, a shameless creature whom, on account of adultery, the Emperor Maximilian had sentenced at Inspruck to be put into a sack and drowned. His wages were eighty ducats a month for himself and ten for his servants, together with clothing, travelling expenses, and provender for three horses.

These indulgences brought immense sums of money into the pope's coffers. For the lie was imposed upon the poor people that whoever purchased a letter of indulgence not only received forgiveness of sins, but also became exempt from all punishment in this life and in purgatory. Hence all classes flocked to the sale; even the poorest spinsters, widows and beggars brought their last piece of money to buy indulgences for the purpose of delivering the souls of their friends from purgatory, so that, if the traffic had not been stopped, Germany would have been left without a penny. And still the pope never had enough, lavishing it not upon St. Peter's but upon his own pride and lewdness. The matter was carried to such extremes that the emperors, kings, princes and lords of the holy empire, as well as others, became displeased, complained of it at several diets, and desired a reformation.— But no one knew any remedy; the earthly god at Rome was too powerful in the Church and in the hearts of men, and his anathema was too much feared to admit of any hope.

As the papal indulgence was so highly prized, the indulgence dealer Tetzel was everywhere received with the greatest pomp. When he entered a town the papal bull was borne before him upon velvet or gilt cloth, and all the priests, monks, council, school-teachers, pupils, men, women and virgins went out in procession, with banners, tapers and songs, to meet him. All the bells were tolled and the organ played, and he was conducted into the church, in the middle of which a red cross was set up, decorated with the pope's arms; in short, God Himself could not have been received with more splendor.

The impudence with which John Tetzel carried on the indulgence traffic was unprecedented. In St. Annaberg he said that if they would speedily buy indulgences all the mountains around the place would become pure silver. In Magdeburg he refused to absolve a rich lady until she had paid a hundred florins. In Leipzig he enticed the people living in the surrounding country by making appointments for his indulgence sermons on Sundays and other holidays, and instituting games in connection with them, such as shooting matches, pole climbing, playing at ten pins for an ox, or dice, or ginger cake, &c. His assistant, Bartholomew Rauch, even surpasssed him. He· said that he could see the blood of Christ flow graciously from the holy red cross upon which hung the pope's arms, and that such great grace had not been bestowed since the time when Jesus suffered. He spoke of the miracles which the cross performed, and excommunicated those who said aught against it.— Tetzel had a regular tariff of sins. Conjuring he forgave for two ducats, polygamy was charged six, murder eight, sacrilege and perjury nine. "With one groat," he said, "you can release the soul of your father from purgatory; and are you so ungrateful as not to wish the deliverance of your father from torture? If you had but one coat you must be moved instantly to take it off and sell it, to secure such grace."

Tetzel threatened that he would have the heads torn off of those who would speak against indulgences, and would thus cast them as heresiarchs into hell. But he was once deceived. When he had gathered a large sum of money in Leipzig, a nobleman came to him and asked him whether he could forgive the sin that he designed to commit; if he could he would give him ten dollars. Tetzel at first declined, and excused himself by saying it was a very important matter; but still he averred that the pope had given him perfect authority to do it, and if the applicant would give him thirty dollars he would grant him the indulgence desired. The nobleman paid this sum, and when Tetzel soon afterwards left Leipzig he lay in wait for him, robbed him of his money, and then told him that this was the sin for which he had purchased indulgence. Tetzel brought complaint against the nobleman, but he was only ridiculed for his levity, and nothing was done.

To show with what diabolical cunning the deceiver belied the poor people, and cheated them out of their money, we add the following incident. After he had offered his indulgences for sale many days at Zwickau and was prepared to leave the place, the chaplains and altarists said to him: "Sir, you are about to depart and we have not enjoyed your indulgences; we would be glad if you would give something for our benefit, that we might be in good spirits on the matter." Tetzel replied that the indulgence money was all packed up, but still he would grant their request. On the following day he ordered the great bell to be tolled, upon which the people flocked to the church in crowds. He then appeared and told them that he had designed to leave that morning, but in the past night a poor soul had moaned so pitifully in the church-yard and cried for help, that it might be delivered from its terrible suffering that he could not help remaining this day. He would now say mass for the soul, and they should in the meantime bring their offerings, that the poor soul might be released from torture. Whoever refused this would prove that he had no sympathy with the poor soul, nay he must himself be immersed in the sin for which the poor soul is suffering; if it be a man he must be an adulterer, if it be a woman she must be an adulteress. That they might be assured that the necessity is great, he would himself make an offering. Thus he was the first to contribute money, and after this there was such a zeal in offering contributions that the people borrowed money of each other in the church for the purpose; for no one wished to be considered an adulterer or adulteress. This money he then gave for the benefit of the clergy, and had a gay time with them afterwards; for the indulgence venders were accustomed publicly to revel in the taverns, and to squander their share of the money in dissipation and debauchery.

In the year 1516 Tetzel finally came also to Juterbock, in the vicinity of Wittenberg. It is incredible what this shameless man was emboldened to pretend and to preach. The pope, he said, has more power than all the apostles, than all the angels and saints, yea, than the virgin Mary herself, for these are all subject to Christ, but the pope is equal with Him. Nay, since the ascension Christ no longer governs the Church, but has committed the government to the pope as his vicegerent. The red cross of indulgence, and the pope's arms hanging on it, should be revered and worshipped as the most holy object. The indulgence renders those who purchase it purer than Baptism, nay, purer than Adam was in the state of innocence in paradise.

"At that time," Luther relates, "I was preacher here in the cloister, and a young doctor fresh from the forge, ardent and joyous in the Holy Scriptures. When people thronged from Wittenberg to Juterbock and Zerbst to obtain indulgences and I, as truly as my Lord Christ has redeemed me, did not know what indulgence was, I commenced preaching with mildness, that something better could be done, something more sure, than preaching indulgences. I had preached before against indulgences in the castle, and had gained little favor at the hands of duke Frederick, who dearly loved his foundation," which had plenary indulgence. Luther advised his hearers rather to give alms to the poor, according to our Lord's command, than to purchase such uncertain grace. He told them that he who repents, receives forgiveness of sins, which Christ has secured by His own sacrifice and blood, and offers and bestows by grace freely and without money.

But Luther with horror discovered, in the confessional, the terrible consequences of the indulgence traffic. The number of his confessors became continually less, and those who came to him declared defiantly that they would not refrain from adultery, fornication, usury and similar sins. As they refused to promise repentance and amendment,

Luther refused to absolve them. Then they appealed to their letters of indulgence. To these Luther paid no regard, but admonished them in the words of our Lord, Luke xiii, 3: "Except ye repent, ye shall all likewise perish." Therefore they returned to Tetzel and told him that this Augustinian monk despised their letters of indulgence. Tetzel became enraged at this, raved, railed and cursed fearfully from the pulpit, and threatened vengeance upon the heretics. To strike terror of his power into the souls of all, he several times had a fire kindled in the market place, thus indicating that he had authority from the pope to burn the heretics, who should oppose the most holy pope and his most holy indulgence.

In the meantime it was reported to Luther that Tetzel had preached the following horrible doctrines: The red cross of indulgences with the pope's arms, erected in the church, is as efficacious as the cross of Christ; he would not exchange his power for that of St. Peter, for he had saved more souls by his indulgences than Peter by his sermons; as soon as the money, paid for the deliverance of a soul from purgatory, rings in the box, the soul leaps up to heaven; the grace of indulgence is the grace by which man is reconciled to God; contrition, sorrow and repentance on account of sin is not necessary, if a letter of indulgence is purchased. In general, Tetzel sought to surpass himself in Juterbock. Among other things he said on the pulpit that on Good Friday he saw the soul of citizen Geserick flying to heaven.

"At that time," Luther tells us, "I did not know for whom the money was intended.— But a book was published with the arms of the Bishop of Magdeburg, in which the questors were commanded to preach these doctrines. From this it appeared that Albert had hired this Tetzel because he was a great brawler; for he had been elected Bishop of Mayence under the condition that he should purchase the pallium at Rome from his own means. There had, within a short period, been three bishops elected at Mayence, Barthold, James and Uriel having died in quick succession, and probably the burden of purchasing the pallium became too heavy for the diocese, as it cost 26,000 florins, some say 30,000; for at such an exorbitant price the most holy father at Rome can sell flaxen thread, which otherwise is scarcely worth a sixpence. So the bishop found out this invention for the purpose of paying the Fuggers, who had advanced the money, by extorting it from the purses of the common people; and he sent this great purse-beater through the country, who threshed away lustily, so that the money fell and leaped and rang in the coffers lavishly. Meantime he did not forget himself. And the pope, too, had his hand in the dish, one half being set apart for the building of St. Peters at Rome. Thus the fellows sallied out joyously and hopefully to beat and thresh the people's purses. This, I say, I did not know then. So I wrote a letter to the Bishop of Magdeburg, exhorting and entreating him to restrain Tetzel and prohibit the preaching of such incongruities, lest evils grow out of it, and reminding him that this would be proper for him as Archbishop. But I received no reply. I also wrote to the Bishop of Brandenburg as ordinary, in whom I had a very gracious superior. He replied that I was attacking the power of the Church and would make myself trouble, and that he would advise me to desist. I can easily conceive that both of them thought the pope would prove too mighty for me, a miserable beggar."

As the bishops would not put a stop to the abomination of indulgences, Luther could no longer keep silence. His divine vocation, as pastor and teacher of the Holy Scriptures, bound him to bear testimony against it.— Thus it was Almighty God Himself who called him to be the reformer of His Church and the antagonist of the papacy. But that he might not be hindered in this holy work God, in a wonderful manner, directed the heart of one who was mighty to favor him.

CHAPTER XV.

THE ELECTOR'S PROPHETIC DREAM OF LUTHER.

On the night of All Saints, before which Luther posted up his theses against papal indulgence, the Elector Frederick the Wise of Saxony had the following dream in Schweinitz, which he wrote down the next morning and, in the presence of the chancellor, communicated it to his brother, Duke John of Saxony.

"As I was lying upon my bed in the evening, somewhat faint and tired, while I was praying, I soon fell asleep and slept soundly and rested comfortably for about the space of two and a half hours; after which I awoke considerably refreshed. I lay upon my bed and had all manner of thoughts, and among other things, I reflected how I might fast to the honor of all the beloved saints, as well as myself and my courtiers. I also prayed for the poor souls in Purgatory, and concluded in my mind to come to their aid and assistance in their flames. I also prayed to God for grace that he might lead me and my counsellors, and my country into all truth and save us, and that He would control by His omnipotent power the evil designs of those who would make our government troublesome.— Being filled with such thoughts soon after midnight, I fell asleep again, and soon commenced dreaming. I dreamed that God sent a monk, with a fine honest countenance to me ;

this monk was the Apostle Paul's natural son, and had for his attendants, by God's command, all the beloved saints, who were to bear witness to the monk, that there was no deception in him, but that certainly he was sent from God; that God commanded me to allow this monk to write something upon the chapel of my castle at Wittenberg; that if I would do so, I should never be sorry for it. I told the monk through my chancellor, that as God had commanded me to let him write, and as he had such powerful evidence, he might write all that he was commanded to write. Immediately the monk began to write and he made his letters so large that I could distinguish them here in Schweinitz. He used a pen so long that the other end of it reached to Rome, and penetrated into the ear of a lion, which lay there, so forcibly that it came out at the other ear, and then extended still further, until it came in contact with the triple crown of his holiness, the Pope, and gave it such a powerful shock that it began to shake, and to fall from the head of his holiness. Your highness and myself stood not far from his holiness at the time; and as his crown was falling, I stretched forth my hand to assist him in keeping it in its place. At this I awoke, holding up my arm, a good deal frightened and angry at the monk because he did not guide his pen more carefully; but upon a little reflection, I found it was a dream. But I was still very sleepy, and soon my eyes were shut again, and

I fell into a sound sleep, and before I was aware of it, the same dream appeared to me again, the second time; for I was again engaged with the monk. I saw how he continued to write; and with the stump of his pen he kept on piercing the Pope through the lion. At this the lion roared most dreadfully, and the whole city of Rome, and all the States of the Holy Empire came running to the place to see what this was. The Pope and the States requested that the monk might be restrained, and that I should be informed of the violence he was doing to his holiness, because this monk was in my country. Here I awoke the second time from my dream and marveled that I had dreamed it again.

"I did not, however, suffer this thing to trouble my mind, but prayed that God would preserve his holiness, the Pope, from all evil; and thus I fell asleep again the third time.— The monk appeared to me again, and I dreamed that the chief States of the Empire, among whom were also I and your highness, proceeded to Rome and endeavored hard to break the monk's pen, and to lead the Pope out of its way; but the more we exerted ourselves to break the pen, the more inflexible it became, the more it rattled and jarred as though it were iron; it rattled and jarred so much that it hurt my ears, and penetrated my heart. Finally I became vexed and tired of it; we gave up, and went away, one after another, and hid ourselves, fearing the monk might be able to do more than eat bread, that he might perhaps do us some harm. Notwithstanding, I caused to be inquired of the monk, how he came in possession of that wonderful pen and what was the reason that it was so tough and solid. He answered, that it was taken from an old Bohemian Goose, (Huss) a hundred years ago, and that an old schoolmaster of his had honored him by presenting it to him, requesting him that, because it was a good pen, he should keep it, and use it in remembrance of him, that he himself also had tempered it; that the reason why it was so strong, was because no man could take away the spirit from it, nor drain the soul out of it, as was the case with other pens. At this he himself was greatly astonished.

"Soon after this a great cry arose, that out of this great pen of the monk, numberless other writing pens had grown in Wittenberg, and that it was amusing to see how learned men strove and contended about it; that part of them thought that, in the course of time, many of these pens would become as inflexible and strong as the one in the monk's hand; and that something remarkable would certainly follow this monk and his pen.

"I now concluded in my dream, to have a personal conversation with the monk as soon as possible. I awoke from my dream and found that it was morning. Wondering at my dream, I reflected upon it, and the fact that it was repeated three times in succession, in one night, made a deep impression on my mind, and I immediately wrote down the principal parts of it. I am convinced that this dream is not wholly without signification, as it was repeated so often."

CHAPTER XVI.
LUTHER'S NINETY-FIVE THESES.—BEGINNING OF THE REFORMATION.

The festival of the dedication of the Castle Church at Wittenberg, as the Church of all Saints, was celebrated on the 1. of November, on which occasion many people were wont to assemble there from far and near. The theses were, according to academic custom, put up on the previous day precisely at the hour of noon. It was on the 31. of October, 1517, that Luther, in the name of God, nailed to the door of that Church his 95 Theses against the abuse of Indulgences. In them he did not yet, however, attack the papal indulgences themselves, but only the grossest abuses practiced in connection with them. Still he thus early admitted that the shameless preaching concerning indulgences rendered it difficult, even for the learned, to defend the Pope's honor and dignity. The first thesis reads thus: "When our Lord Jesus Christ said, Repent ye, His will was that the whole life of His believers on earth should be a constant, unceasing repentance." He further maintains: "Every true Christian, whether living or dead, is a partaker of all the blessings of Christ and the Church by the gift of God, even without indulgence," and thus confesses that faith alone justifies before God and saves. This was the doctrine for which thousands of anxious souls who were tormented by doubts had long since deeply sighed. Hence it was that in a few days the Theses had spread over all Germany, and in a few weeks were read with avidity throughout all Europe. In four years a traveller purchased them in Jerusalem. It was as though the angels had become messengers and borne them before the eyes of all men. No one believes what a noise they made, and nearly every person was pleased with them.

When the pious monk, Dr. Fleck, found these theses posted up at Steinlausig and had read a portion of them, he exclaimed in the height of his joy: "Ho, ho! this man will accomplish it: he comes, upon whom we have waited so long." He then wrote a very consoling letter to Luther and exhorted him to go on in good cheer, as he was on the right path, and God and all the prayers of the captives in the Romish Babylon would be with him. But others were dismayed. The celebrated Dr. Albert Kranz of Hamburg, who received Luther's Theses upon his death-bed a few days before his decease, exclaimed: "Go to your cell, good brother, and pray: Lord have mercy upon me," by which he meant that the poor monk could not possibly succeed in his battle against the mighty Pope. An old clergyman of Hoxter in Westphalia said: "My dear brother Martin, if you can abolish purgatory and the papal hawking and huckstering you will be a great hero indeed!" Luther's prior and sub-prior also were alarmed, and entreated him not to bring disgrace upon their order. He replied: "Dear fathers, if the work is not begun in God's name, it will soon come to naught; but if it is begun in His name, let Him do as seems to Him good." "Then they were silent," Luther subsequently related, "and the work has gone on until now, and shall go on, if God please, more bravely still until the end, Amen!"

In thus attacking the heart of the papacy by his Theses, without in the least designing it, Luther was not prompted by any carnal impulse. He himself says of it: "Who was I, a miserable and despised brother, looking then more like a corpse than a man, that I should set myself against the majesty of the Pope, who was a terror not only to the kings of the earth and to the whole world, but also to heaven and hell, if I may so speak, and at whose nod all must obey. What and how my heart suffered in that first and second year, and in what humility, which was not false or feigned, but most real, I would almost say in what despair, I labored, about this the secure spirits who afterwards with great pride and presumption attacked the majesty of the Pope, know, alas! but little."

CHAPTER XVII.
NEGOTIATIONS WITH CAJETAN AND MILTITZ.

The Theses of Luther had produced a mighty commotion in the hearts of all. Prierias, Eck, Emser, Tetzel, &c. attacked him in hostile publications, in which they sought to defend indulgences. But by Luther's testimony a constantly increasing multitude was gained for the truth.

At first the pope treated the whole affair with contempt, and thought that the controversy would cease without any interference on his part. Rut when he saw that his authority was waning on account of it, he on the 15. of July, 1518, cited Luther to appear personally at Rome within sixty days. Through the Elector's influence it was arranged, however, that Luther should have a hearing in Germany before the papal legate, Cardinal Cajetan, at Augsburg, where a diet was then in session. Luther was warned not to leave Wittenberg, as men of power were lying in wait for him to strangle or to drown him. But he said that he was not conscious of teaching anything but the pure theology, and that he long since knew his preaching would be a stumblingblock to the holy Jews and foolishness to the wise Greeks. He accordingly, in September, proceeded to Augsburg on foot, and reached Weimar on the 28th, where he passed the night in the cloister. When the purveyor of the monks, John Kestner, said in compassion:

"My dear Doctor, the Italians are learned men, and I am afraid you will not be able to maintain your cause before them : they will burn you on account of it," Luther replied : "With nettles it might pass, but with fire it would be too hot. Dear friend, in a Lord's Prayer entreat our dear Father in heaven in behalf of me and His dear child Christ, whose is the cause which I advocate, that He may be gracious to Him. If He only maintains His cause, mine is maintained ; but if He will not maintain it, I assuredly cannot maintain it for Him, and His will be the dishonor."

Luther arrived in Augsburg on the 7. of October, and wished to proceed at once to the legate ; but the councilmen, to whom Luther had been recommended by the elector, opposed it, because they knew that the legate was bitterly hostile to Luther. They therefore sought to procure for him a safe-conduct from the emperor, but obtained it only after three days, as the emperor was absent. Meantime the servants of the cardinal came daily and said: "The cardinal offers you every favor, why do you fear? He is a very kind father." But another whispered in his ear : "Do not believe it, he never keeps his promise." On the 9. the orator of the Margrave of Montferrat, Urban, sent Luther word that he should not go to the legate without first having conversed with him. He then visited Luther, having, according to the general opinion, been appointed by the legate himself, and urged him with great prolixity and, as he said, with the most salutary counsels, simply to coincide with the legate, return to the Church, and recant his errors. He earnestly advised Luther not to defend himself, and said: "Would you enter the lists?" Luther: "If I can be convinced of having said anything different from the sense of the holy Roman Church, I shall immediately condemn myself and retract." "Oh, ho!" he repeated, "you intend to enter the lists." He then gave utterance to some most absurd propositions, and admitted that it is allowable to preach false opinions, if they only prove advantageous and fill the coffers, but maintained that no dispute concerning the pope's power could be tolerated, and that all must submit to his command, even in matters of faith. On the third day he came again and reproachingly asked him why he did not come to the cardinal, who was graciously waiting for him. Luther replied that he must follow the advice of the honorable men, to whom he had been recommended by the elector, who were all of the opinion that he should not go without a safe-conduct, but that he would go as soon as this were received. Urban was irritated at this and said: "Do you think that the elector will hazard his dominious on your account?" Luther: "That I do not at all desire." Urban: "But where will you take refuge then?" ·Luther: "Under the heavens." Urban: "If you had the pope and the cardinals in your power, what would you do?" Luther: "I would show them all respect and honor." Upon this Urban bit his finger, after the fashion of the Italians, and said "Hm, ha, ha!" and came no more.

On the 12. of October the hearing finally commenced. The legate represented to Luther that he had taught the following two errors: first, that the treasure of indulgence is not the merits or the sufferings of our Lord Jesus Christ, and secondly, that a person desiring to receive the holy sacrament of the altar must have faith of his own: these errors he should recant. Luther adduced the proof orally and in writing, from the Holy Scriptures, that man is justified alone by faith in God, and that he becomes worthy to receive the sacrament alone by faith in the words of Christ; but the legate paid no attention to this. On the third day indulgences were the subject of conference. The legate cried incessantly that Luther should recant. The latter sought ten times to speak, but every time the cardinal thundered away to drown his voice. Finally Luther also spoke in loud tones, but with due reverence, saying: "Most worthy father! your highness must not suppose that we Germans know nothing about Grammar. To have a treasure and to acquire a treasure are two different things." The legate then arose in anger and said: "Go, and let me not see you again unless you recant." So Luther departed from the cardinal's presence.

The latter, in the afternoon, assigned to

Staupitz the task of inducing Luther to recant. Staupitz confessed his inability to do it, as Luther was too well versed in Scripture for him. He finally consented, but when Luther entreated him to put a different interpretation upon the Scriptures adduced if it were possible, he acknowledged that he could not. He himself said to Luther at the time: "Consider, dear brother, that you have begun in the name of Jesus." Staupitz then desired the cardinal again to confer with Luther, but Cajetan replied: "I have no desire to dispute further with this beast, for he has penetrating eyes and wonderful thoughts revolve in his head."

Upon this Luther addressed a humble letter to the cardinal, in which he declared his readiness to recant everything as soon as he could be convinced of having erred; but he received no reply. In a subsequent letter he respectfully took leave of the cardinal, and again expressed his willingness to submit to the judgment of the Church, but added with boldness that, by the grace of God, he now had less fear of punishment than of errors in matters of faith. As he still received no answer, the silence of the legate began to seem suspicious to him and to all his friends. Violence was apprehended. He therefore hastened away from Augsburg on the 20. of October, having left an appeal *a papa male informato ad papam melius informandum*, that is, from the pope badly informed to the pope to be better informed. Dr. Staupitz furnished him

with a horse, the council secured for him a
guide who was acquainted with the roads, and
Christopher Langemantel assisted him to make
his way out of the city, at night, through a
narrow gate. Thus he rode eight German
miles on the first day, and when he reached
the inn, in the evening, he was so weary that
after dismounting in the stable he was unable
to stand, and immediately fell upon the straw.
In Græfenthal he was overtaken by count
Albert of Mansfeld, who laughed at his horse-
manship and constrained him to become his
guest. On the 31. of October he again arrived
at Wittenberg in good health.

When the legate heard that Luther had departed, he became very angry and wrote to
the elector that he should send Luther to
Rome, or at least banish him from his dominions. Others, however, advised the contrary.
Thus the excellent Bishop of Wuerzburg,
Laurentius of Bibra, wrote: "Let your highness by no means dismiss the pious Dr. Martin, for injustice is done him." Even the
emperor Maximilian sent a message to the
elector expressing the wish that he would take
good care of the monk, as he might yet be
needed.

The pope now plainly saw that Luther's
doctrine could not be suppressed by violence.
He therefore resorted to measures of mildness,
and sent his chamberlain, Charles of Miltitz,
as nuncio to the elector to present to him the
consecrated golden rose, which, however, was

only ridiculed. This Miltitz, in January, 1519, had a consultation in Altenburg with Luther, in which he entreated Luther to assist in making peace, and promised that he would use his influence with the pope to the same end. Luther consented to everything as far as he could without violating his conscience and sacrificing truth. They finally agreed that both parties should in future keep silence and Luther should address a humble letter to the pope.

Luther relates that Miltitz was really commissioned by the pope to bring him as a captive to Rome, but that God defeated him on the way, that is, he was deterred by fear on seeing the multitudes who were favorable to Luther. He therefore exchanged his violent purpose for an artful pretence of benevolence. "But he betrayed himself and showed what he had purposed in his heart when he said to me: 'O, dear Martin, I thought you were an old, decrepit theologian, who sat behind the stove and disputed ; but I see you are yet a young man, fresh and vigorous. I would not undertake to bring you away from Germany even though I had with me an army of 25,000 men; for on my journey I embraced the opportunity to ascertain how the people are disposed toward you and what they think of you, and I have learned at least this much, that where there is one on the pope's side there are three on yours against the pope'."

So they parted on very friendly terms. On

the evening before, Miltitz had Luther take supper with him, admonished him with tears, and dismissed him with a kiss; but Luther considered this a Judas kiss, and says that he acted also on his part as if he did not understand these Italian arts and crocadile tears. Upon this the nuncio summoned the shameless bawler Tetzel into his presence and commanded him to stop his indulgence traffic. Tetzel was so terrified that he died soon afterwards; and no one pitied the miserable creature, who was now forsaken by God and men, except Luther, who wrote him a letter of consolation and preached to him also the grace of God.

In accordance with his promise Luther wrote a humble letter to the pope, wherein he yet said: "Most holy Father! I declare in the presence of God and all His creatures, that I never desired and do not now desire to infringe, either by force or stratagem, the power of your holiness and of the Roman Church. Nay, I freely confess that the authority of this Church is over all, and that nothing in heaven or on earth should be preferred over it, except Jesus Christ alone, who is Lord of all." Luther would thus gladly have had peace, but his enemies soon drew him, against his will, into the contest again, and in its progress it became ever clearer to him that the pope is the predicted Antichrist.

CHAPTER XVIII.
THE LEIPZIG DISPUTATION.

Dr. Carlstadt had taught, like Luther, that man's free will can, without grace, do nothing but sin, and had, on account of this doctrine, entered into a dispute with Dr. John Eck.— By the intervention of Luther they now agreed to settle the controversy in a public disputation. Eck published the propositions upon which he intended to dispute with Carlstadt; but in these he artfully directed his principal blows at Luther himself. He says in them: "It is not in accordance with the Scriptures, nor with the holy fathers, to say that Christ's words, Repent ye, meant to render the whole life of believers a continual repentance." In the 13. thesis he declared it to be a necessary article of faith that the pope is, by divine right, the vicar of Christ and the successor of Peter.

Thus Luther was compelled to appear himself and defend the truth against Dr. Eck.— On the 24. of June, 1519, Luther with Dr. Carlstadt, Philip Melanchthon, Dr. John Lang and Nicholas Amsdorf came to Leipzig, accompanied by several hundred Wittenberg students armed with spears and halberds, who walked beside their carriages. The discussion was held in the castle of Pleissenberg, the largest hall of which duke George had beautifully decorated for the purpose. All the seats and tables were hung with gorgeous tapestry.

The space allotted to the Wittenbergers was adorned with the portrait of St. Martin, that assigned to Dr. Eck with a picture of St. George. At the opening of the discussion, Peter Mosellanus, Professor of Eloquence at Leipzig, delivered a Latin address on the true method of disputing. When he had closed, the halls resounded with the "Come, Holy Spirit, God the Lord," whilst the whole assembly reverently knelt. A great multitude of persons had gathered together. To preserve order a guard of armed citizens, with banners flying, were in daily attendance at the castle.

Eck disputed first with Carlstadt on the freedom of the will, afterwards with Luther on the primacy of the pope. He maintained that the pope is, by divine right, the head of the Christian Church. Luther replied that the Christian Church must undoubtedly have a head, but this head is Christ, not the pope. If the pope were the head of the Church, the Church would, at the death of a pope, be without a head until another is elected. The Eastern Church never acknowledged the pope, but is not on that account heretical. The pope is primate only by human right. Eck sought by all means in his power to have Luther suspected of the Bohemian heresy. Luther warded off such suspicions, maintaining that the Bohemians did wrong by arbitrarily rending the unity of the Church. When he further declared that there are among the articles of

Huss, or of the Bohemians, some which are quite Christian and evangelical, duke George shook his head, placed both hands on his hips, and said in a tone loud enough to be heard by the whole audience: "The plague take it!"

The Bohemians soon afterwards actually entered into an alliance with Luther who, on the 3. of October, 1519, received letters from two Hussite ministers of Prague, the pastor John Paduschka and the provost Wenceslaus Rosdialovinus, of the College of Emperor Charles. In these they state that they had read his writings with pleasure, and exhort him not to neglect the grace of God, which is upon him for the salvation of many, and to bear willingly the reproach of Christ. They assure him that there are in Bohemia many precious believing souls who support him with their prayers night and day. The former made him a present of knives, the latter of a book of John Huss, remarking: "This one thing I know, that what John Huss once was in Bohemia, that you, Martin, are in Saxony."

CHAPTER XIX.

Luther burns the Papal Bull.

Eck had flattered himself that he would triumph over Luther, but he sustained a disgraceful defeat. Filled with rage he hastened to Rome to seek revenge. At this period, Luther wrote the two celebrated works: "To the Christian Nobility of the German Nation on the Reformation of Christianity," and "Of the Babylonish Captivity of the Church," in which with holy zeal, and with ever increasing clearness, and decision, he exposed and attacked the abominations of the papacy.

Charles of Miltitz tried once more to reconcile Luther with the pope. Luther dedicated to the pope his masterly work on the "Liberty of the Christian," which, on the 6. of September, 1520, he sent to him, accompanied by a letter full of reverence for his person. "It is true," he says in it, "I have boldly attacked the Roman court, which you yourself must confess, as no man on earth can do otherwise, to be worse and more shameful than ever Sodom, Gomorra and Babylon were; and as far as I can see, there is no hope and no help for its wickedness. In the meantime you, Holy Father Leo, sit like a sheep among the wolves, and like Daniel among the lions, and Ezekiel among the scorpions. What can you do alone against so many wild monsters?" He then declared that he would have kept his promise to remain silent had not Eck's stupid ambition drawn him into the discussion.

In the meantime Eck had succeeded at Rome in inducing the pope to issue a bull, dated June 4., 1520, in which 41 propositions extracted from Luther's works were condemned, his writings were ordered to be burnt, and sentence of excommunication was pronounced against him as a heretic, if he did not recant within 60 days. Eck carried the bull through Germany in triumph. In the hereditary domain of the emperor he actually succeeded in having Luther's works committed to the flames, but in many places, especially in electoral Saxony, he was received with universal derision. In Leipzig, where he at first made a pompous display of his bull, and boasted that he would now teach Martin something, he fared so badly that he was compelled to seek refuge in the Paulinian cloister and dared not show his face again.

Luther continued in good cheer, notwithstanding his condemnation by the pope. He wrote to a friend: "I have now much more courage, since I have become certain that the pope is plainly the Antichrist and Satan's seat." He wrote a work "Against the bull of the Antichrist," in which he says; "If the pope does not revoke and condemn this bull, and punish Dr. Eck and his associates, its advocates, no one shall doubt that the pope is the enemy of God, the persecuter of Christ, the disturber of the Church, and the real Antichrist. For hitherto such a condemnation of the Christian faith publicly professed, has never been heard as is uttered in this infernal, accursed bull."

Thus Luther was forcibly ejected from the Romish Church, because he had confessed the pure doctrine of God's word. He therefore desired to show the whole world what he thought of such an excommunication. On the

10. of November, 1520, at 9 o'clock in the morning, a fire was kindled at the Elster gate of Wittenberg, and, in the presence of a large assembly of doctors, masters and students, Dr. Luther cast the bull which had been sent him, together with the papal Canon Law, into the flames, saying: "Since thou hast vexed the Holy One of God, may the everlasting fire vex and consume thee!" On the following day he earnestly admonished his hearers to guard against the papal decrees, saying: "If you do not with all your heart contend against the scandalous government of the pope, you cannot be saved." He then, in a tract, laid before the public his reasons for taking this step and showed, at the same time, what ungodly propositions are contained in the papal Canon Law, among which are these: "The pope and his court are not obliged to submit to the laws of God. If the pope were so wicked as to lead innumerable souls to hell, no one would have a right to reprove him for it."

CHAPTER XX.

LUTHER GOES TO WORMS.

In the year 1521 the German Emperor Charles V. held his first diet at Worms. The elector asked Luther whether he would appear if he were cited by the emperor, to which he replied: "In humble obedience I am ready to present myself at the approaching diet of

Worms and, by the help of the Almighty, so to conduct myself that all men may see that in what I have written and taught I was not moved by an inconsiderate, disorderly and wanton obstinacy, nor by a thirst for temporal honor or profit, but that my desire was, as a poor teacher of the Holy Scriptures, according to my conscience, my oath and my duty to glorify God, to promote the salvation of Christians, to benefit the whole German nation, to extirpate dangerous abuses and superstitions, and to deliver the whole Christian Church from endless burdens and blasphemies." And to Spalatin he wrote: "If I am cited, I purpose to go; if I cannot go in good health, I will go there sick; for if the emperor calls me I cannot doubt that it is the call of God. If they then use violence we must commend the matter to God. He who preserved the three men in the fiery furnace of the king of Babylon, still lives and reigns. Here you have my mind and my resolution. Expect everything of me, only not flight or recantation. 1 will not fly, much less recant. The Lord Jesus help me! For I can, without injury to the cause of piety and the salvation of souls, do neither."

On the 26. of March the herald of the emperor, Caspar Sturm, who was to accompany Luther, brought him the imperial citation to appear at the diet within 21 days. His friends represented to Luther the great danger which he was about to meet, warning him that, because there were so many cardinals and bishops at Worms, they would forthwith commit him to the flames, as they did Huss at Constance. But he answered: "And if his enemies built a fire which should extend from Wittenberg to Worms and reach to the heavens, he would, having been cited, appear in the name of the Lord, and enter the jaws of Behemoth, confessing Christ and letting Him rule." "I do not think of flying," he wrote to Spalatin, "and leaving the word of God in danger, but intend to confess it unto death, the Lord being merciful to me and helping me." Thus he joyfully entered upon his journey, accompanied by Justus Jonas, Nicholas Amsdorf and Jerome Schurff, a celebrated lawyer, and commended himself everywhere to the prayers of Christian people. On the way he preached to vast assemblages of people at various places. Satan, indeed, sought in every possible manner to hinder his progress. During the whole journey he was unwell, as he had never been before. In Eisenach he became so sick that fears were entertained for his life. He was doomed, too, to see the messengers, who were sent to post up in all the towns the imperial mandate condemning Dr. Martin.— His principal enemies, moreover, who dreaded his appearance in person, took pains to keep him away, using sometimes threats and sometimes flattery. But still the faithful hero remained fixed in his resolve. "Christ lives," he wrote from Frankfort, "therefore we shall enter Worms in spite of the gates of hell and the powers of the air." Even at Oppenheim yet, he received an anxious letter from Spalatin, earnestly warning him not to come to Worms. He replied, "And if there were as many devils in Worms as there are tiles upon the houses, still I would enter it."

Thus on the morning of April 16. Dr. Luther, clothed in a monk's gown, entered Worms in an open carriage, accompanied by three others. Before him rode the imperial herald in his official vestments, bearing the eagle escutcheon upon his breast, attended by his servant. Many noblemen and courtiers rode out to meet him. When he drove into the city, the Duke of Bavaria's jester, Cochlæus, met him with a crucifix in his hand, and, whether instigated by another or moved by a spirit of prophecy, addressed him with the words; "Now thou art come, thou expected one, for whom we have been waiting in the darkness." More than two thousand persons attended Luther to his lodgings, where many princes, counts and lords, temporal and spiritual, visited and conversed with him until night. The young landgrave Philip of Hesse, also rode up to see him, and upon taking leave he extended to him his hand and said: "If you are in the right, Doctor, God help you!"

CHAPTER XXI.
LUTHER AT THE DIET.

Early the next morning the marshal of the empire, Ulrich of Pappenheim, visited Luther and communicated to him the imperial order that he should appear at the diet in the afternoon at 4 o'clock. So the decisive hour was near at hand when the faithful witness of Jesus Christ must appear before the mighty of the earth. But Luther did not put his trust in men, he leaned alone upon God, whose grace and help he implored in a fervent prayer, which was heard by several persons and taken down, as follows:

"Almighty, eternal God, what a vain thing is the world's grandeur, yet how greatly do men prize it, and how little faith have they in God! How frail and weak is the flesh, and how powerful and active, through his apostles and the worldly-wise, is Satan! How swiftly does it apostatize and pursue the beaten track, and the broad road to perdition, the reward of the ungodly; looking only at what is splendid and powerful, grand and mighty, honored and respected! Truly, if to such things I too must look I am undone, the hour of my destruction is come, my doom is fixed. O God, O God, O Thou my God, Thou my God, do Thou stand by me, and support me against the combined reason and wisdom of the world; do Thou do it, Thou must do it, Thou alone. It is not my cause, truly, but Thine;

I have nothing personally which could bring me in contact, and engage me with these great lords of the world. Truly, I too would prefer happy, quiet days, and an undisturbed life. But the cause is Thine, O Lord and it is righteous forever. Support Thou me; I confide not in men, but in Thee, Thou faithful, eternal God. All is vanity and trifling; the flesh, and all that savors of the flesh is deceitful. O God, my God, dost thou not hear, my God? Art Thou dead? No, Thou canst not die; Thou only hidest Thyself. Hast Thou chosen me for this, I ask Thee, as I am sure Thou hast, then do Thou direct all; for I never, in all my life, thought or intended to be opposed to such great lords. Do Thou, then, my God, assist me in the name of Thy beloved Son, Jesus Christ, who shall be my shield and protection, yea my strong fortress, through the power and strengthening influences of Thy Holy Spirit. Lord where dost Thou remain? Thou my God, where art Thou? Appear, appear! I am ready, even to lay down my life, patiently like a lamb. For the cause is righteous, and it is Thine, neither will I ever separate myself from Thee. Be this resolved in Thy name: the world, with all its fiendish might, shall still leave my conscience untrammelled. And if my body, notwithstanding it is the workmanship of Thy hands, and Thy creature, should perish, and perish utterly, (against which, nevertheless, Thy Word and Spirit assure me) the soul is Thine, it belongs to Thee, and will remain Thine forever. Amen. God help me! Amen."

As soon as four o'clock arrived Luther was brought to the diet. Immense multitudes of people crowded around to see the monk, some even climbing to the roofs of houses for this purpose, so that it was necessary for the marshal of the empire to conduct him through private gardens and houses in secrecy, in order to reach the hall. When he was about to enter the council Hall, an old General, George of Freundsburg, laying his hand on Luther's shoulder, said: "My poor monk, my poor monk, you are now upon a march such as I and many a captain have never, in our severest campaigns, entered upon; but if you have the truth and are sure of it, go forward in God's name, and fear nothing; God will not forsake you!" The door was opened and Luther stood before the emperor and the realm. It was the largest and most brilliant assembly of the German Estates that had been held for a long period. Besides the emperor upon his throne, there was present his brother, the Archduke Ferdinand, six electors, twenty-four dukes, eight margraves, thirty-six bishops, one papal and five royal ambassadors, and upwards of two hundred others of high rank. In the antechamber and at the windows, about five thousand persons were congregated.

Luther was first asked whether he acknowledged the books, which lay upon a bench, to be his, and then whether he was willing to recant their contents. The first question, the titles of the books having been read, he answered in the affirmative. In regard to the second, as it pertained to faith and salvation, he asked time for consideration. This was granted until the following day. He was then conducted back to his lodgings by the marshal of the empire. On the way the people cheered him, and a voice cried: "Blessed is the womb that bare thee!" Many brave men of the nobility also visited and encouraged him, saying: "Doctor, how is it? it is said that they intend to burn you; but this shall not be; rather should they all perish with you." But Luther trusted alone in God.

When, on the following day, he had been again brought before the diet and was asked whether he would defend all his books, or whether he was willing to recant anything, he greeted the assembly reverently, and stated that in all that, in the simplicity of his heart, he had taught and written, he sought only the glory of God and the welfare and the salvation of souls. He then expressed himself more particularly upon the contents of his books. In some he had taught the word of God in its purity; in others he had attacked the papacy and the doctrine of the Papists; in the others he had written against individual defenders of the papal tyranny, in which he had no doubt been more severe than was meet, as he was no live saint. "But," he continued, "as I am a mere man, and not God, I cannot otherwise defend my books than my Lord and Savior did His doctrine, who said: 'If I have spoken evil, bear witness of the evil.' If the Lord, who knew that He could not err, refused not to hear testimony against his doctrine, even though borne by a wicked servant, how much more should I, who am but dust and ashes, and who may easily err, be willing to hear if any one would bear witness against my doctrine. For this reason, by the mercy of God I conjure you, Most Serene Emperor, and you, most illustrious Princes, and all men of every rank, whoever may be able, to testify against me and prove from the writings of the prophets and apostles that I have erred. As soon as I am convinced of this I will retract every error, and will be the first to throw my books into the fire. What I have just said, plainly shows, I hope, that I have carefully weighed and considered the danger and the character of the dissension which has arisen on account of my doctrine, and of which I was yesterday earnestly admonished. To me it is a source of the greatest joy to see that the Gospel is the occasion of trouble and dispute, for this is the nature and destiny of the word of God, as our Lord Himself says: 'I came not to send peace on earth, but a sword; for I am come to set a man at variance against his father,' &c.— Therefore it should be well considered that God is wonderful in His counsels and judgments, lest that which is done to allay dissensions proceed from confidence in our own strength and wisdom, and, by persecuting the word of God, we draw down upon ourselves a terrible deluge of insurmountable dangers. Besides this, we should be concerned not to have the reign of this good and noble youth, the emperor Charles, not only not to begin, but not to continue and end in unhappy troubles. For it is God who taketh the crafty in their own cunning and removeth the mountains and they know not. Therefore it is necessary to fear God."

This, and much besides, Luther said not in a boisterous manner, but modestly and deferentially. At the close of his address, which lasted two hours, he was quite exhausted.— But the emperor did not fully understand the German, and therefore desired Luther to repeat his speech in Latin. "I was in a great perspiration," he himself relates, "and was very warm on account of the tumult, and because I stood among princes. Then Frederick of Thunan said to me, 'If you are unable to do it, Doctor, it is enough.' But I repeated all my words in Latin." Now, however, a clear and concise answer was demanded to the question whether he would recant or not, Luther said: "Since your most serene Majesty and your high Mightinesses require from me a clear, simple and precise answer, I will give you one with neither horns nor teeth, and it is this: unless I am convinced by the testimony of the word of God, or by clear and cogent reasons, as I cannot submit my faith to the pope nor to the councils, which have manifestly often erred and contradicted themselves, and as I am bound in conscience by the passages which I have quoted, I cannot and will not recant anything, for it is neither safe nor right to do anything against conscience. Here I stand; I cannot do otherwise; God help me! Amen."

Luther was then led away by two men.— This occasioned a tumult, and the knights inquired whether they were leading him away as a prisoner; but Luther replied that they were merely accompanying him. While he was pressed by the crowd, duke Eric of Brunswick sent him a silver flagon filled with Eimbeck beer, with the request that he would refresh himself with it. Luther replied: "As duke Eric has this day remembered me, so may our Lord Jesus remember him in the hour of his departure," which words the duke remembered in his last struggle. When he entered his lodgings the Spaniards ridiculed him; but he was so bold and so joyful in the Lord that he said to Spalatin and others: "If I had a thousand heads I would rather have them all severed from my body than recant."

Deep was the impression which the powerful address of Luther, so full of faith, made upon the whole assembly. Many were gained for him and his cause. The emperor, however, declared: "This man shall not make a heretic of me." The papists were enraged that liberty had been granted him to defend himself at such length. Many urged the emperor to condemn him notwithstanding his safe conduct. But the emperor replied: "We should keep our promises, and if faith and honor were banished from the whole world, we should expect to find them in the German emperor." Even duke George of Saxony, Luther's bitterest enemy, declared that it would not accord with ancient German customs to break the plighted faith. The elector had heard Luther with great favor. With deep joy he said to Spalatin on the same evening: "Oh how well Martin conducted himself! what a beautiful address he delivered, both in German and Latin, before the Emperor and all the estates! he is much too bold!"

Further efforts were made to induce Luther to recant, but all in vain; he referred to the words of Gamaliel: "If this counsel or this work be of men, it will come to nought; but if it be of God ye cannot overthrow it." The emperor then ordered him to return home, protected by his safe conduct, within 21 days. Luther replied: "As the Lord hath pleased so hath it come to pass: blessed be the name of the Lord." He then again declared to the emperor and the estates that he had desired nothing but that "a reformation according to the word of God might be effected, for which he had so earnestly prayed." On the 26th of April, 1521, he departed from Worms, preceded by the imperial herald.

CHAPTER XXII.

LUTHER AT THE WARTBURG.

The most of the Estates had already left Worms when the imperial decree, called the edict of Worms, was issued on May 26, pronouncing in the most venomous terms the ban upon Luther and his defenders, and ordering the destruction of his books.

Meantime Luther and his companions were on the way to Wittenberg. In Eisenach he preached, then visited his relatives in Moehra. On the 4. of May he took leave of them to continue his journey by way of Altenstein. But as he drove through a narrow pass in the vicinity of this castle, suddenly two knights with their attendants sprang upon them, ordered the driver to halt, pulled Luther with great violence from the carriage, dressed him in a horseman's garb, put him upon a horse, and dashed away into the forest, whilst his terrified companions were permitted to proceed. They rode about the forest for several hours until, about midnight, they reached the strong mountain castle of the Wartburg, near Eisenach.

This was done at the command of the elector, Frederick the Wise of Saxony, who desired to secure Luther against his foes. The latter finally yielded to the elector's prudent counsels, although he would much rather have shed his blood as a testimony to the truth, and remained 10 months at the Wartburg, where he was known by the name of Yonker George. The news of his capture spread with great rapidity. It was reported that he had fallen into the hands of his enemies. Many lamented him as though he were dead, while his enemies rejoiced.

The silence and solitude of his Patmos, as, referring to Rev. i, 9, he called the Wartburg, were of great benefit to him; for here he could devote himself to the word of God without interruption. This external quiet was, indeed, painful to him. "I would rather," he says, "burn upon glowing coals for the honor of God's word, than rot here half alive."— But he was resigned to his lot, because he saw it to be the will of the Lord. "I am a singular prisoner," he wrote, "who remain here not only voluntarily, but also involuntarily; voluntarily, because my Lord wills it thus ; involuntarily, because I would gladly preach the word of God among the people." He suffered while here not only from repeated attacks of painful sickness, but also great mental anguish. He complained of want of zeal in prayer, of indolence, of drowsiness, and of many other evils, so that he was tempted to think that God had forsaken him. "Here I sit," he writes, "and all the day long picture to myself the Church, and deplore my insensibility, because I do not dissolve in tears and pour forth from mine eyes streams of sorrow for the slain of my people." He was troubled by Satan, moreover, not only with the severest internal struggles, but also with external terrors, which he conquered, however, by despising them. His confession, in this regard, is remarkable, that such crosses are much heavier to bear is solitude than among friends, who can support and comfort us with the word of God.

Notwithstanding these difficulties Luther displayed unparallelled activity. He studied Greek and Hebrew with great assiduity, preached diligently to his associates, wrote numerous spirited letters to his friends, and prepared many valuable works for the Church. He translated into the German language the whole New Testament, which was published in the following year, and circulated in a short time through all Germany. Even mechanics and women read it so eagerly that they gradually committed it to memory, and in the course of a few months were able to dispute with the priests and confute them with the word of God. He also wrote the first part of his Church Postill and a work "On Spiritual and Monastic Vows," which he dedicated to his dear father. In the latter he proves clearly from the word of God that the vows which are taken without, yea, against the word of God, are not binding upon the conscience of a baptized Christian.

During Luther's absence, the cardinal Albert of Mayence had again ordered the preaching of indulgences at Halle. Luther wrote a tract "Against the Idol at Halle," and wrote to the Elector that if he did not, within 14 days, abolish the abomination of indulgences he would publish his treatise and show to the world the difference between a bishop and a wolf. The elector answered graciously that the sale of indulgences had been stopped, and that he would in future show himself to be a pious, spiritual prince.

Amid so many labors Luther needed recreation. In the pleasures of great lords and idle people, as he called those of the chase, he seldom took part. Sometimes he visited good friends in the neighborhood, who often failed to recognize him as he appeared in the dress of a knight, with a long beard and with a sword at his side. In such excursions he was accompanied by a discreet cavalier, whose faithful admonitions not to lay aside his sword and take up his books as soon as he entered a house, lest he should be taken for a priest, he subsequently often praised. But his church and pulpit at Wittenberg were constantly in his mind, so that once at table the words escaped him: "O, that I were at Wittenberg." He also once, in November, secretly visited his friends there, and having enjoyed himself in their company for several days, he returned to the Wartburg.

CHAPTER XXIII.
Luther returns to Wittenberg.

By the instrumentality of Luther the happy sound of the Gospel had gone forth into every land. Satan had indeed sought, by means of the pope, emperor and learned men, to suppress it, but it continued to spread all the more rapidly. He then adopted another plan to crush the truth : he excited disturbances in Luther's own congregation. During Luther's absence, but with his consent, the Augustine monks had abolished the papal mass and had introduced the true Christian mass, or the Holy Supper of the Lord. But Dr. Carlstadt, in whose estimation the reformation was progressing too slowly, instigated the students to a scandalous licentiousness, who, in the rudest and most violent manner, assaulted the mass in the parochial church. At the Christmas festival he and his adherents cast the pictures and crucifixes out of the church and burnt them, dashed the altars to pieces, abolished the candles, hymns and ceremonies, rejected the use of chalice and patens, went to communion without previously announcing themselves or being examined, and helped themselves to the host. They did this from sheer audacity, without having instructed the people by preaching, without the consent of the government, and without caring that offence was given to the weak. They claimed that the first commandment and Christian liberty impelled them to this course, and that they were filled with the Holy Spirit; and they condemned all as heretics who differed with them. Carlstadt even declared all science superfluous, desired to be no longer styled doctor, but simply neighbor Andrew, and advised the students to go and learn trades. One of his most resolute followers, the rector of the boys' school, went so far as to call from the school window to the assembled citizens that they should take their children away from school. Moreover, fanatics came to Wittenberg from Zwickau, who boasted that they were called by a clear voice of God to teach, that they had familiar conversations with God, that they could see into the future, in short, that they were prophets and apostles.

Luther sought to allay these disturbances by writings, but in vain; they became constantly worse. Things came to such a pass that only those were considered Christians who ridiculed the priests, ate meat on Friday, pulled down pictures, &c. Then his congregation in a letter earnestly entreated Luther to come back. He was under the ban of the pope and the interdict of the emperor; the elector had given him permission only in extreme necessity to return to Wittenberg, because he could not protect him there; but in spite of all dangers he hastened to Wittenberg, early in March, 1522. To pacify the elector he wrote to him a letter full of the joyous heroism of faith: "It must be so if we would have the word of God, that not only Annas and Caiphas rage, but also that Judas appear among the apostles and satan among the Sons of God." "I am conscious that if matters stood in Leipzig as they do in Wittenberg, I would go there though it rained duke Georges nine days incessantly, and each one were nine times more furious than duke George."— "These things are written to your electoral Grace in the assurance that I go to Wittenberg under much higher protection than that of the elector. I do not intend either to ask your Grace's protection. Nay I hold that I can protect your Grace rather than your Grace can me. Indeed, if I knew that your Grace could or would protect me I would not come. In this matter no sword shall or can assist: God alone must help here, without all human care and aid. Therefore he who believes most can here afford most protection."

As soon as Luther reached Wittenberg, on the 7th of March, he attacked the fanaticism of Carlstadt with the word of God, and by means of eight sermons, delivered in as many consecutive days, he restored the peace of the Church. He then told his hearers that they were wanting in the fruit of faith, charity, which patiently bears with the neighbor's infirmities, and kindly instructs him, but does not gruffly snarl at him. External improvements, he tells them, are very well, but they must be introduced in order, without tumult and scandal, not too hastily. "Because I cannot pour faith into the heart," he says, "I cannot and should not force any person to it, for it is God alone who causes it to live in the heart. To force it by law only produces a sham, an external thing, an imitation, a human ordinance, the result of which is nothing but saints in mere semblance, or hypocrites.— For in this case there is no heart, no faith, no love. We must first gain the hearts of the people, which is done by using the word of God, preaching the Gospel, showing the people their errors. He that will heed it let him heed it; he that will not, remains without.— Iu this way one receives the Word into his heart to-day, another to-morrow, and so they turn away from the mass, of themselves.— Thus God accomplishes more with His Word than you and I and all the world could accomplish with our force combined. For God takes possession of the heart and so the whole man is gained; then the evil must fall and be abandoned of itself." Even Carlstadt, whom Luther treated with great forbearance, now kept quiet for several years, although in his heart he harbored a bitter grudge against Luther. The Zwickau prophets withdrew from Wittenberg, but, in their rage against Luther for despising their spirit, they wrote him a letter full of abuse and execration.

CHAPTER XXIV.
THE PEASANT WAR.

These heavenly prophets, also called Anabaptists, now scattered the poison of their fanaticism among the people with the greatest zeal. The most active among them was Thomas Muenzer, with whom Carlstadt, who introduced the soul-destroyiug error that Christ's body and blood are not substantially present in the Holy Supper, associated himself in 1524. By their atrocious sermons they deceived the people to such an extent that they not only fell away from the word of God, but also rebelled against the government.— To check their violence Luther himself went about preaching to the people, but only with partial success. In Orlamuend the rage of the populace against him was so great that he was compelled to flee, while some followed him with the execration: "Depart in the name of a thousand devils, and may you break your neck before you get out of the city."

As early as 1524, the peasants in Suabia had revolted, and the flame of rebellion, in 1525, spread through Franconia along the Rhine, and thence nearly over all Germany. The peasants had banded together to form what they called a Christian Union, had stated their grievances in 12 articles, and had chosen Luther as arbiter. He declared many of their demands just and reasonable. In their first complaint they asked for the congregations the right to elect their own pastors. In regard to this Luther said: "This article is just. The right of electing pastors you cannot with any semblance of justice deny. To this no government can or should be opposed. Nay, the government must not prohibit each one's teaching and believing as he chooses, provided that he does not teach disorder and revolt." But he at the same time shows them what a heinous sin they commit by rising against the civil authorities: "You say that the government is wicked and intolerable, forbidding you to have the Gospel, oppressing you in temporal things, and thus ruining you in body and soul. Answer: the wickedness and injustice of the government does not justify conspiracy and rebellion. I say this, my dear friends, faithfully to warn you, that in this affair you must cease to use the Christian name and boast of Christian right. For no matter how just your cause is, it befits not a Christian to quarrel and fight, but he must suffer the wrong and bear the evil. This cannot be changed. 1 Cor. vi, 7 Because you are determined to defend your own cause and will not bear violence and wrong, you may do and omit what God permits; but the Christian name, the Christian name, I say, leave that unsullied, and use not that as a cloak of your impatient, contentious, unchristian proceeding. For Christians do not maintain their cause with the sword and rifle, but with the cross and suffering, as their captain, Christ, does not bear the sword, but hangs upon the cross.— Hence too, their victory does not consist in ascendency and power, but in submission and weakness." But just as sharply Luther rebuked the ungodly tyranny of the princes. "In the first place we have no person on earth to thank for these disorders and disturbances but you princes and lords, especially you blind bishops and stupid priests and monks, who in your obduracy do not cease to this day to rave and rage against the Holy Gospel, although you know it to be true and cannot confute it. And in the civil government you do nothing but practice extortion to pamper your pomp and pride, until the poor common people cannot and will not bear it any longer.— For this, my dear sirs, you must know, that God so directs events that your madness cannot, and will not, and should not be endured always. You must amend and let the word of God have its way; if you will not do it voluntarily by peaceful means, you must do it ruinously by means of violence." "It is to me a source of the greatest sorrow," he says to the princes and peasants, "so that I would give my life to have it otherwise, that two inevitable evils must result on both sides. For as neither party could engage in the contest with a good conscience it must follow, in the first place, that those who are slain are eternally lost in body and soul, as they die under God's wrath without repentance and without grace, and there is no help for it. For the lords would be fighting to maintain their tyranny and their persecution of the Gospel, and their oppression of the poor, or to aid those who are engaged in this wickedness. This is abominable injustice, and those who are guilty of it must be eternally lost. On the other hand the peasants would be fighting to defend their revolt and their abuse of the Christian name, which is also fighting against God, and those who die in such a contest must also be eternally lost, and there is no help for it."

Luther admonished the government to adjust the matter amicably with the peasants.— He also went himself to Thuringia for the purpose of preventing, by his preaching, the outbreak of a rebellion, twice endangering his life in the effort. But the peasants despised his faithful counsel, and everywhere raged furiously. They robbed, plundered, laid waste, burnt, and murdered wherever they appeared, destroying above 200 castles and many cloisters. Upon their enemies they took most bloody vengeance. For example in Weinsberg they impaled 70 knights amid the most horrible tortures. Then Luther issued his very severe tract "Against the rapacious and murderous Peasants," in which he counselled the government once more to offer the insurgents an amicable settlement, and if this should be of no avail, to put them down with the sword. Thus the peasants were routed everywhere by the princes. Thomas Muenzer, the servant of the servants of God with the sword of Gideon, as he called himself, was defeated on the 5. of May, 1535, near Frankenhausen; of his band, consisting of 8,000, some were slain and the rest made prisoners; he himself was beheaded.

CHAPTER XXV

Luther's Marriage.

According to the laws of the pope, none of those who have taken so-called spiritual orders, such as monks, nuns, priests, &c., are permitted to marry. Luther on the contrary proved from the word of God that matrimony is a divine institution, and that all men are at liberty to marry; he also advised others to enter the matrimonial state. But as for himself, he wrote yet in 1524: "I have no disposition to marry, because I stand in daily expectation of being executed as a heretic." But God ordered otherwise. On the 13. of June, 1525, he was married to Catherine von Bora, who, having become convinced of the propriety of the step, by reading Luther's writings, had left the cloister two years before. Luther was prompted to this by the wish of his aged father, and by his desire to confirm his teaching by his practice. He himself testifies that God suddenly and wonderfully led him into matrimony, while he was engaged in other thoughts; "for," he says, "I feel no carnal love and longing, but have a delight in matrimony as an institution and order of God." The papists of course were highly offended at the monk's marrying a nun ; but Luther was unconcerned about them, saying, in the confidence of faith : "I would cheerfully give them more offense if I only knew something more that would please God and mortify them."

In his married life Luther sought to exemplify all that he had taught in this regard, endeavoring as a true bishop to rule his house well. He and his wife cordially loved and honored each other. God gave them six children, John, Elizabeth, Magdalene, Martin, Paul, Margaret—three sons and three daughters. His children, in his manifold cares and anxieties respecting Church affairs, afforded him great delight ; he loved them tenderly, brought them up in the nurture and admonition of the Lord, and daily repeated with them the Ten Commandments, the Creed and the Lord's Prayer ; he also frequently sported with them and became a child among the children. Thus he addressed the following letter to his little son John when he was four years old :

"Grace and peace in Christ ! My dear little son : I am glad to see that you learn well and pray diligently. Go on in this way, my boy ; when I come home I will bring you something pretty. I know of a beautiful, happy garden in which there are many children with golden coats who gather nice apples under the trees, and pears, and cherries, and plums, and who sing and skip and are merry. They have pretty little ponies, too, with golden bridles and silver saddles. I asked the man to whom the garden belongs who these children are. He said they are the children who love to pray and learn and who are pious. Then I said: Dear man, I also have a son and his name is Johnny Luther; may he not come into the garden too, and eat of these nice apples and pears, and ride these pretty ponies and play with these chidlren? And the man said: if he is a good boy and loves to pray and to learn he may come, and Lippus and Jos too; and when they all come together they shall also have fifes, tymbals and lutes, and all kinds of music on stringed instruments, and shall dance too and shoot with little crossbows. And he showed me there a little meadow in the garden arranged for dancing, and it was hanging full of golden fifes, tymbals and nice silver cross-bows. But it was early and the children had not had their breakfast yet, so I could not stay for the dance, and I said to the man : My good Sir, I will go right away and write all this to my dear little boy, Johnny, so that he may pray diligently and learn well, and be pious, that he may come into this garden. But he has an aunt Lena, whom he must also bring along. Then the man said : it is all right; go and write so to him. Therefore Johnny, my dear little boy, learn and pray with good cheer, and tell Lippus and Jos to learn and pray also, then you will all go into the garden together. With this I commend you to Almighty God. Greet aunt Lena and give her a kiss for me. In the year 1530. Your dear father, Martin Luther."

At the same time Luther was very strict with his children. When his son John was 12 years old he once committed a wrong, on account of which Luther for three days refused to have anything to do with him, notwithstanding that he humbly asked forgiveness in writing. And when his mother, Dr. Jonas and Dr. Teutleben interceded for him, Luther said, "I would rather have my son dead than disobedient. St. Paul did not without reason say that a bishop must rule his own house well and have obedient children, that other people may be edified through them, follow their example and not be offended. We ministers are honored so much that we might set a good example. But our untrained children cause others to take offense and bad boys commit sin in virtue of our privileges."

Luther's house was not exempt from the cross. Once his dear wife was at the point of death, but God heard his prayers in her behalf. With many tears he saw two of his dear daughters depart this life, Elizabeth in her first, and Magdalene in her fourteenth year. For the latter he wrote the following epitaph :

"I, Lena, Dr. Luther's daughter, here
Am laid with saints to rest till Christ appear,
I who, from my first breath,
Had been an heir of death,
Now live, and all is well forever,
Since Thou, O Christ, didst me deliver."

CHAPTER XXVI.
THE MARBURG CONFERENCE.

When the Reformation began, all who received the Gospel were perfectly united in the pure doctrine. Carlstadt was the first who introduced dissension by teaching that the body and blood of Christ are not truly present under the bread and wine. This error was adopted also by Ulrich Zwingli, pastor at Zurich in Switzerland, who maintained that the words, "this is my body" meant no more than "this signifies my body." As the poison of this error kept spreading constantly further, Luther preached and taught against it with earnestness and with severity; for a severe wound requires a sharp knife. In 1527 he wrote the excellent book "That the words, 'This is my body' still stand firm against the fanatics," and in 1528 his "Large Confession concerning the Holy Supper." But the Zwinglians continued in their error and subsequently separated from the Church of the pure faith and organized a Church of their own, called the Reformed. For the purpose of removing this dissension, the landgrave Philip of Hesse arranged a colloquy between the contending parties, which took place in Marburg on the first three days in October, 1529. Among others, Luther, Melanchthon and Jonas were present of the one side, and Zwingli and Œcolampadius of the other. In the first place Luther urged against the opponents that they not only teach false doctrine concerning the Eucharist, but that they also inculcate the following errors: That Christ is not true, essential God; that original sin is not sin; that original sin is not forgiven in Holy Baptism; that the Holy Spirit is not communicated by the word and the sacraments; that justification takes place not only by faith, but also by works. Luther and his coadjutors instructed them on these points and they yielded in all of them.

Upon this the Reformed endeavored to prove that in the Holy Supper the body and blood of Christ are not present. The first argument adduced by Œcolampadius was that our Lord says, in John vi, 63, "the flesh profiteth nothing," and therefore there can be no flesh in the sacrament, as the fleshly reception would be without profit. Luther replied that Christ does not here speak of His flesh, for He says before that His flesh imparts eternal life and that His flesh is meat indeed; but He refers to our flesh and calls that unprofitable, as is evident from the antithesis: "it is the Spirit that quickeneth;" it would be

9*

dreadful to say that the flesh of Christ profiteth nothing.

The second argument of the Reformed was drawn from reason. They maintained that a body could not be in two places at the same time and that accordingly, as the body sitteth at the right hand of the Father in heaven, it could not be present in the sacrament on earth. Luther replied that the reason of man cannot judge the power and glory of God; that Christ has assumed the human nature, which must therefore, according to the Scriptures, have part in the Divine attributes and glory; and that consequently the human nature of Christ must be omnipresent, and His body and blood can accordingly be present in the Holy Supper.

Zwingli answered that God does not ask us to believe absurdities. To this objection of unbelieving reason Luther answered in the power of faith: "What God speaks is always for our salvation, even though He should command us to eat crab apples or pick up straws." When Zwingli still persisted in maintaining it to be absurd that such a great miracle should be performed by wicked priests, Luther explained: "This is not done by the merits of the priest, but according to Divine order. It is done because Christ commanded it.— Thus it is to be held concerning the power of the word and all the sacraments that they are powerful and produce their effect not by the merit and holiness of the priest or minister, but by the power of God's ordinance and commandment. To maintain that the sacraments are not efficacious when administered by wicked priests, is a Donatistic error." To this clear account of Luther Zwingli made no reply.

A transition was then made to the third argument, which Œcolampadius presented thus: "The sacraments are signs, and therefore they must signify something; hence we must conclude that the body of Christ is here merely signified, not present." Luther had at the beginning written the words of our Lord: "This is my body," upon the table before him, as his firm and sure ground. He admitted that the sacraments are signs; "but," he said, "we must not interpret them otherwise than our Lord. That the sacraments are signs means especially that they signify the annexed promises. So circumcision signifies especially the word which is annexed, that God will be gracious. If any one should seek another signification, as that circumcision signifies the mortification of the flesh, it would be futile whilst he despises the promise signified, which is the chief signification. Therefore we must not deal wantonly with significations, but observe how God's word explains itself."

But when Luther saw that the opponents persisted in their opinions with increasing tenacity, he closed the conference on his part, thanking Zwingli and Œcolampadius that they had conducted the discussion so kindly. But he added, at the same time, that as they would not dismiss their opinions he must commit them to the judgment of God and pray that He would enlighten them and bring them back into the way of truth.

The landgrave was an attentive listener during the whole discussion, and, convinced of the arguments for the truth, he said publicly: "Now I shall believe the simple words of Christ rather than the acute thoughts of men." Œcolampadius, also, as Selnecker relates, experienced qualms of conscience on account of his error. For when the landgrave said to him: "Doctor, the Wittenbergers after all stand on sure texts; you have nothing but comments and explanations; and if the others have better ground than you, why do you hesitate?" he answered with a sigh: "Gracious lord, I would that this hand had been taken off before I had written a word upon the subject."

The landgrave, however, urged that an agreement should be made before they separated. Zwingli approached with tears in his eyes and declared: "God knows there is no man in the world with whom I would rather agree than with you, Luther, and your Wittenbergers." He and the others of his party offered to teach, with Luther and his friends, that the body of Christ is really present in the sacrament, but in a spiritual manner, if these would then recognize them as brethren. Luther then replied: "I also desire to be in conflict with no one; but God's word and the truth must be more precious than all the world's friendship." He further said to them, "You have a different spirit from ours," and censuringly asked them how they could consider him and his friends brethren while they considered them in error; he regarded this as a sign that they did not deem their tenets very important. Thus the Reformed, as Luther said, had to leave the field as heretics; for as they would not submit to the truth, the Lutherans could not have fraternal fellowship with them. But they extended to the opponents the hand of peace and charity, as Luther writes, so that the harsh writings and words might cease, and that each might present their own doctrine without railing, though not without refutation and defence.

It was in this year also that Luther wrote his Smaller and Larger Catechisms, of which Matthesius justly said: "If Dr. Luther had done nothing more than write these Catechisms, the whole world could never sufficiently thank him for it."

CHAPTER XXVII.

THE PRESENTATION OF THE AUGSBURG CONFESSION.

As religious affairs were to be considered at the Diet of Augsburg, the elector of Saxony appointed Luther, Melanchthon, Jonas and Bugenhagen to draw up a brief and clear summary of the principal doctrines of the Christian faith. This was done in a document, the basis of which were 17 articles previously prepared by Luther. This was subsequently still further developed by Melanchthon, with the consent of Luther and the other confessors, and thus originated the Augsburg Confession, concerning which Luther says: "I have read the Apology of Philip from beginning to end; it pleases me exceedingly well, and I know of nothing by which I could better it, or change it, nor would I be fitted to do it, for I cannot move so moderately and gently. May Christ our Lord help, that it may bring forth much and great fruit, as we hope and pray. Amen."

Before his departure the elector ordered prayers in the Church throughout his province for a prosperous issue of the Diet. When the theologians declared to him that they would rather appear before the emperor alone and present their cause, that he might not be endangered, he answered: "God forbid that I should be excluded from your company; I will confess my Lord Christ with you." Melanchthon, Jonas and Spalatin went with him to Augsburg, whilst Luther remained at the castle Ehrenburg, near Coburg.

On the 15th of June, the evening before the festival of *Corpus Christi*, the emperor, in great pomp and glory, entered Augsburg.— That very evening yet he desired of the evangelical princes that they should take part in the Corpus Christi procession on the following day. But these princes positively refused, declaring that they were not disposed by their participation to encourage such ordinances, which are manifestly in opposition to the word of God and the command of Christ.— And when the emperor persisted in his demand the evangelical margrave, George of Brandenburg, solemnly declared: "Rather than deny my God and His Gospel, I would kneel here before your Majesty and have my head severed from my body." The emperor graciously replied: "Dear prince, not head off, not head off!"

So the ever memorable day approached on which the little band of Lutherans should confess the Lord Jesus Christ. On the 20th of June the elector John the Constant invited his brethren in the faith to his rooms and earnestly exhorted them to stand firm. "All counsels that are against God," he said, "must come to naught, and the good cause must finally triumph, as is certain from the Scriptures, Is. viii, 9." Early on the following morning, alone in his closet, he prepared himself, by the reading of Psalms and earnest prayer, for the important step.

The emperor had finally consented that the Confession of the Evangelicals should be publicly read. On Saturday, June 25th, 1530, at 3 o'clock in the afternoon, the Diet assembled in the episcopal palace, the chapel of which was selected for the reading of the Confession. The highest dignitaries of Christendom are present, and the German emperor Charles V., presides, whose dominion extends from the North to the South of Europe, and across the ocean to Peru and Mexico in America. The electors, prelates, princes and estates of the German nation have assembled, and foreign nations have sent their envoys and the pope his legates, to hear that Confession. The Evangelical confessors, the elector John the Constant with his excellent son, the electoral prince John Frederick, the margrave George of Brandenburg, the dukes Ernest and Francis of Lueneburg, the landgrave Philip of Hesse, the prince Wolfgang of Anhalt, and the delegates of the cities of Nuremburg and Reutlingen now joyfully arise, and in their name the two electoral chancellors, Dr. Brueck and Dr. Baier, the former with the Confession in Latin, the latter in German, proceed to the middle of the room. The emperor asks that the Latin copy be read; but the elector John replies that they are upon German ground, and he hopes that his majesty will permit them to use the German tongue. And now, while the assembly is all attention, Dr. Baier reads the Augsburg Confession in German so slowly and so loudly that the multitude congregated in the courtyard could distinctly understand nearly every word.

Even the emperor, as well as the papistic estates, were moved by this glorious Confession. Their opinion that the Lutherans renounced the ancient Christian faith, was at once refuted. The emperor had the information conveyed to the Protestant princes that he had graciously heard their confession of faith. Duke William of Bavaria could not refrain from addressing the elector in friendly words after hearing the confession. To Dr. Eck, who was present with them, he said reproachfully: "Luther's doctrine had been represented as far otherwise than I have just heard in their Confession. You have consoled me with the assurance that their doctrine could be refuted." When Eck replied: "I would undertake to refute it with the fathers, but not with the Scriptures," the duke answered: "I understand it then: the Lutherans are entrenched in the Scriptures, and we are aside of them." The learned bishop Stadion of Augsburg publicly acknowledged: "What has been recited is the pure plain truth, and we cannot deny it." Even the violent persecutor of the Gospel, duke Henry of Brunswick, invited Melanchthon to dinner. "I rejoice," says Luther, that I have lived to see the hour in which Christ is publicly preached by his confessors, before an assembly so illustrious, in this glorious Confession. Herein is fulfilled what the Scripture saith: 'I will declare thy testimonies in the presence of kings.' Yea, that will also be fulfilled which follows: 'and shall not be put to shame.' 'For he that confesses me before men,' says He who cannot lie, 'him will I also confess before my Father who is in heaven.'" Spalatin also calls it "a confession the like of which has not been heard not only for a thousand years, but not since the world exists. In no history and in no ancient father is anything like it to be found." And in the same spirit Matthesius testifies : "Since the days of the apostles there has never been a greater achievement and a more magnificent confession than that which was made before the whole Roman empire at Augsburg." It was soon translated into many languages and spread, in transcribed and printed copies, over all lands. Many were thus brought to an acquaintance with the Lutheran doctrine, and perceived its agreement with the Holy Scriptures and the doctrine of the ancient Church, and joyfully embraced it. For the Augsburg Confession is a pure, correct and incontrovertible confession of the Divine truth of Holy Scripture ; hence also, it is the flag around which all true Lutherans in all lands rally ; and the Lutheran Church until this day recognizes only those as her members who, without any reservation, accept all the articles of the unaltered Augsburg Confession. The papistic theologians, at the command of the emperor, prepared a work in which they endeavored to refute this Confession ; but Melanchthon victoriously defended it against their attacks in the "Apology," which the Evangelical Lutheran Church also adopted as one of her confessions.

 In the meantime Luther was not idle in Coburg, but took an active part in all the proceedings. He gave to his friends at Augsburg good Christian advice, rich consolation and great encouragement. He also wrote a number of excellent works, among others an exposition of the 118. Psalm, which he called his favorite Psalm because it had ministered comfort to him in so many troubles. The 17. verse of this Psalm : "I shall not die, but live, and declare the works of the Lord," he wrote upon the walls that he might always have it before his eyes to comfort him. At this time, also, he composed, on the basis of the 46. Psalm, his song of victory : "A safe stronghold our God is still," together with the melody, and he sang it daily. He also frequently received absolution and the holy communion.

Above all, Luther prayed diligently that the Gospel might triumph, although to mere reason this seemed at that time an impossibility ; for Satan and the Romish Antichrist had armed themselves terribly against the Gospel and were determined to destroy it at all hazards. On the pope's side were arrayed the powerful emperor and the mightiest kings and princes of the earth, and the pope and his cardinals, bishops, monks and learned men exerted all their powers to induce them to exterminate the Lutherans. It thus seemed certain that the little band of evangelical confessors would be overthrown. But Luther prayed all the more fervently that the Almighty would help them. "For inasmuch as this Diet," writes Matthesius, "was directed chiefly against Dr. Luther's doctrine, and against those who assisted in preaching this doctrine, or who in their dominions and cities adopted it as true, as the books of the Roman doctors in reference to this matter clearly demonstrate, our doctor was also at his post, like Moses when he sent his faithful servant Joshua to war against king Amalek. For Dr. Luther also held in his hand the staff and rod of God, and came before the face of God, and, in the knowledge of the Lord Jesus Christ, lifted up his holy and weary hands, with which he had severely borne down and weakened the papacy, and cried day and night to God that He would maintain the honor of His name, His holy Gospel and kingdom, and preserve in the true faith and pure doctrine the true Joshuites and German knights, who, together with the angels, were at Augsburg waging war against Antichrist, and that He would strengthen and comfort them with His Holy Spirit, and guard them and protect them by His holy angels; as also all true Christians at that time, in the whole Roman empire, in all the schools and churches, faithfully assisted Dr. Luther and his friends with their cries and sighs; and indeed Christ, the only Protector and Guardian of His Church, upon whose word, blood, merits and oath Dr. Luther laid his hands, and based and offered up his prayer, also assisted with earnest and unspeakable sighs, repeating His eternal prayer before His God and Father."

Veit Dietrich, Luther's associate at Coburg, thus wrote to Augsburg, to his teacher Melanchthon concerning it: "I cannot sufficiently admire this man's noble constancy, joyful courage, faith and hope in these distressing times; but he also incessantly sustains them by a careful consideration of God's word. No day passes on which he does not spend at least three hours, and these the most suitable for study, in prayer. Once I had the good fortune to hear him pray; O what faith was there in his words! He prayed with such reverence that it was manifest he was speaking with God, and yet again with such faith and such hope that it seemed as if he were speaking with a father or a friend. 'I know,' said he, 'that Thou art our God and Father. I am certain, therefore, that thou wilt bring to nought the persecutors of Thy children; if thou dost not do it, the danger is Thine as well as ours.— Surely the whole matter is Thy own; we have been constrained to enter upon it; it is for Thee to protect it.' Thus I heard him pray in a distinct voice, while I stood at a distance. My heart also burned within me with great zeal, when I heard him addressing God so confidently, so earnestly and so devoutly, and in his prayer so urgently insisting upon the promises in the Psalms, as being certain that that for which he prayed would be accomplished. Therefore I doubt not but that his prayer will be of great service in the desperately difficult business of this Diet."

Luther at the same time wrote the most powerful letters of consolation to his friends at Augsburg. He assured the elector that it was a sign of God's love to him that He granted him His word so richly and deemed him worthy to suffer reproach and enmity on account of it. "Besides this," he continued, "a merciful God shows Himself even more gracious by causing His word to be so mighty and fruitful in the dominions of your electoral grace. For truly in the dominions of your electoral grace are to be found more and better pastors and preachers than in any other country in the world, who most faithfully preach the pure doctrine and assist in preserving so admirable a peace. The tender youth, male and female, now grow up so well instructed in the Catechism and the Scriptures, that my heart delights to behold how the boys and girls are able to pray, to exercise their faith, and to speak more of God and of Christ than all the inmates of convents, cloisters and schools formerly could, or can even now.— Truly, such young people form a beautiful paradise in the dominion of your electoral grace, the like of which there is not in the world besides. And all this God has done in the vicinity of your electoral grace, as an evidence that He is graciously disposed towards your electoral grace. As if He would say: 'Behold, dear duke, I here commit to thee my noblest treasure, my delightful paradise; thou shalt preside over them as a father, for under thy name, protection and government I wish them to be, and I confer the honor upon thee to be my gardener and steward.'"

Melanchthon was especially in need of his encouragement, as he was at that time tormented with cares. Luther wrote to him that he hated such cares exceedingly. "That they thus rule in your heart," he said, "is caused, not by the greatness of this business, but by the greatness of our unbelief. But let it be as great as it may, He also is great who conducts it, and from whom it proceeds, for it is not our cause. Why therefore do you thus incessantly torment yourself? If the cause is false, let us recant; but if it is true, why charge Him with falsehood who with so many promises commands us to be quiet and calmly to wait? 'Cast thy care upon the Lord,' He tells us. What can the devil do more than kill us? Christ has once died for our cause, but for righteousness and truth He will not die; on the contrary, for this He lives and rules."

When Melanchthon, notwithstanding this, continued to fear and grieve, Luther cheered him with the words: "Grace and peace in Christ! I scarcely know, dear Philip, what to write to you, so greatly perplexed am I on account of your unhallowed and foolish cares, for I know that I preach to deaf ears. The cause is that you, to your great injury, believe only yourself, and not others. I can say with truth that I have been in greater distress than, I trust, you ever will be, and I wish no man, not even those who rave so much against us, even if they are knaves and tyrants, to become equal to me in this. And notwithstanding this I have often, in such distress, been comforted through the word of a brother, now through Pommer's, now through yours, now through Jonas' or another's. Therefore do you also hear us, who do not speak according to the flesh or the world, but undoubtedly according to God through the Holy Ghost.— Though we are insignificant, beloved, do not on any account let Him be insignificant who speaks through us. Is it then false that God has given His Son for us? Then may the devil or one of his creatures be a man in my stead. But if it be true, why do we then burden ourselves with pernicious fears, trembling, anxiety and sadness? Just as if He would not be with us in these little things, when He, nevertheless, has given His Son for us, or as if Satan were mightier than He. I know to a certainty that our cause is right and true, yea, that it is the cause of Christ and of God Himself, who have no sins to blush for, as I, poor sinner must blush and tremble. Therefore I am an entirely calm spectator, and do not at all regard the threatenings and ravings of the papists. If we fall, Christ falls with us, He, the Ruler of the world; and if He fall, I would sooner fall with Christ than stand with the emperor. Therefore I pray you, for Christ's sake, not to discard the divine promises and consolations when he says: 'Be of good courage, I have overcome the world.'— It is not false, of that I am assured, that Christ has overcome the world. Why, therefore, do we fear the vanquished world as if it were the vanquisher? May the Lord Jesus sustain you, that your faith may not fail, but increase and obtain the victory.''

To the chancellor Brueck he wrote in the joy of faith, the following letter: ''I recently witnessed two miracles. In the first I beheld, through the window, the stars in the heavens, and the whole beautiful arch of God, and yet nowhere perceived any pillars upon which the Architect had based such arch; yet did the heavens not break down, and this arch still stands firm. Now, there are some who search for the pillars, and would like to touch and to feel them. But because they cannot do this they tremble with fear, as if the heavens would certainly fall, for no other reason than that they cannot touch or see the pillars. If they could touch these the heavens would stand firm In the other I beheld great, dense clouds hanging over us like a mighty ocean, and yet I saw no base for them to rest upon, and no vats in which they were contained; still they fell not, but merely grimly greeted us and fled away. When they had passed away there shone forth both the base and our roof, which had borne them up, the rainbow. That, truly, was a frail, slight, insignificant.

base and roof, so that it also disappeared in the clouds, and seemed more like the shadowy images seen through painted glass than such a mighty base, thus causing one almost to despair as much of the base as of the great mass of water. Nevertheless it was evident that this apparently frail image bore up the mass of water and protected us. Yet there are some who more regard and fear the mass and heaviness of water and the clouds, than this frail airy image ; for they would like to feel the power of this image, and because they cannot do this, they fear that the clouds will cause an eternal flood. Thus I have been constrained in a friendly way, to jest with your honor, and yet to write in seriousness ; for it afforded me especial joy to learn that your honor was more than all the rest of good courage and unwavering confidence in this our hour of trial.

When the papists negotiated with our people respecting an agreement in doctrine, Luther faithfully warned his friends. To Spalatin he wrote : "I understand that you have reluctantly undertaken the strange task of uniting the pope and Luther ; but the pope, I ween, will be unwilling, and Luther begs to be excused. Have a care that you do not ignobly lose your labor. If you accomplish the matter in opposition to both, then I shall soon follow your example and unite Christ and Belial. In short, this negotiation concerning union in doctrine displeases me, for such union is wholly impossible as long as the pope will not abolish his papacy."

He was pleased with Melanchthon that he had not admitted it to be a matter of indifference, but a command, to receive the Lord's Supper under both kinds. "For it is not in our power," added he, "to establish or to tolerate anything in the Church of God, or in the divine worship, which cannot be defended by the Lord's word. The shameful word indifferent my soul loathes; yea, with this word we can easily make all commands and institutions of God indifferent; for if we once permit anything to be indifferent in God's word, how shall we prevent the rest from becoming indifferent?"

But complaints again reached him concerning his friends at Augsburg, especially concerning Melanchthon, as if, for the sake of peace, they had conceded too much. Luther admonished them: do not by any means suffer divisions to arise among you. Let peace be esteemed by us as much as it may, yet is the Lord of peace and the umpire in the war greater than peace and more to be honored. Our duty is not to be apprehensive of future war, but our duty is simply to believe and to confess." But the suspicion was unfounded, and the Lord heard the prayer of Luther that He would conduct the confessors back in health and strength.

On the 14th of September, to Luther's great joy, duke John Frederick, with count Albert of Mansfield, unexpectedly arrived at Coburg. He presented Luther with a gold ring. "But I was not born to wear gold," said Luther, "for it immediately fell from my finger to the ground, (it being somewhat too large,) and I said : Thou art a worm and no man. It should have been given to Faber or Eck.— Lead suits better for thee or a rope around the neck."

The duke wished to take Luther with him, but the latter begged him to let him remain there that he might receive his friends on their return, to wipe the sweat from their faces after such a warm siege. He hoped also soon to see them delivered, and thought they had done enough. "You have confessed Christ," he wrote, "offered peace, born enough calumny, and have not returned evil for evil ; in short, you have worthily performed the holy work of God, as it becomes His saints. Rejoice now in the Lord, and be joyful, ye righteous ; look up, and lift up your heads, for your redemption draweth nigh. I will laud you as faithful members of Christ, and what further renown do you want ? Or is it a small matter faithfully to have discharged the duties of Christ's office, and to have shown yourselves His worthy members ? Be it far from you to esteem the grace of Christ so lightly. But more when we meet."

Finally he had the pleasure of greeting the dear confessors in Coburg. He congratulated his elector that by the grace of God he had been delivered from the hell at Augsburg. On the way home he with his companions stopped with Spalatin in Altenburg. As Melanchthon there wrote at table, Luther arose and, taking from him his pen, said: "We serve God not only by labor, but also by quiet and rest; therefore he gave the third commandment and enjoined the Sabbath."

CHAPTER XXVIII.
REFORMATORY LABORS.

Upon Luther's return to Wittenberg he was required, notwithstanding his bodily infirmity, to perform an extraordinary amount of labor. The question was again agitated whether Lutheran princes and estates could, in case of necessity, form a religious league. Luther did not favor it, because those who enter into such alliances usually put their trust in men, for which reason also the prophets of the Old Testament had so zealously opposed them.

In the year 1531 Luther issued a warning to his dear Germans that they should not aid in opposing and suppressing the pure doctrine of the Gospel. This publication made such an impression even upon the emperor, that in 1632 a general national peace was concluded, towards the attainment of which the elector John in particular largely contributed. By the death of this prince which occurred shortly afterwards, the Lutheran Church was again thrown into deep mourning. He fell asleep in the presence of Luther, with the same confession of Christ which he had made two years before in Augsburg. Of this, as well as of his other virtues, Luther, in the two funeral sermons which he devoted to his memory, presents many remarkable evidences.

Luther now continued without change to proclaim the word of the Lord, and published in this year also several beautiful works.— Among these were his very valuable summaries of the Psalms, which he wrote with incredible rapidity, the whole having been completed in 16 hours. What a brave soldier of Christ he was is shown in his sermon on Eph. vi, concerning "The Armor and Weapons of Christians;" and with what eloquence he eulogized the excellence of charity is evinced in his tract on 1. John iv.

As Luther had heard that the preachers at Frankfort on the Maine taught Zwinglian doctrine respecting the sacrament, pretending that there is no difference between this and Luther's doctrine, and that they also rejected confession, he wrote, in 1533, the powerful and conclusive "Warning to the Frankfurters to beware of Zwingli and Zwinglian doctrine," at the close of which, giving instruction concerning confession, he says: "If thousands of worlds were mine, I would rather lose all than permit one jot of this confession to be banished from the Church."

To the Lutherans who, at this period, were fiercely persecuted and banished by duke George, Luther addressed several letters of consolation; and as this prince charged him with perjury and rebellion, he defended himself with vehemence and with a just zeal like Elijah's.

In the year 1534 Luther, by the special assistance of God, completed the great work of translating the whole Bible into the German language. This work he had commenced in 1517, when he translated the seven penitential Psalms, and upon it he was diligently engaged 17 years, devoting to it a large portion of his time. The difficulties which he had to encounter in this work transcended all conception. In the Old Testament, especially, these were so great that he often sepnt four weeks in reflection and inquiry upon a single word, before he was satisfied how it should be translated into the German. It is therefore with justice that Matthesius calls this translation of the Bible one of the greatest wonders which God accomplished through Dr. Luther, so that it seems to an attentive reader as if the Holy Spirit, by the mouths of the prophets and apostles, had spoken in our German language. This translation surpasses not only all that had been made previously, which had, moreover, become very scarce, and which were unintelligible, but also all that were made subsequently, even down to the present day.

In this respect, also, Luther must ever remain the master, and to his work must be allotted the prize. God richly blessed this work; for by the millions of copies of this translation the word of God was scattered not only over all Germany, but by translations made from it into other languages it was also spread over other lands. By this translation, moreover, a rich treasury of language was supplied, from which the peculiar and energetic language of the Church was derived, as this is found chiefly in Luther's works, by which, again, a good foundation was laid for the development of the German language in general.

In 1535 the Anabaptists created new troubles and deceived many persons. They rejected the written word of God and the ministerial office; they maintained, in a blasphemous manner, that nothing but bread and wine is distributed in the Holy Supper; they reviled the government and led a rude, scandalous life. They carried on their abominations especially in the city of Muenster, until their heretical proceedings were checked by force of arms. Against these enemies of the Christian Church, also, Luther, in a number of treatises, vigorously wielded the sword of the Spirit, which is the word of God, and faithfully warned against their errors, as he did also against the sneaks and hedge-priests, who presume to teach without a regular call.

At the close of this year a papal legate, whose name was Paul Vergerius, appeared in

Germany for the purpose of announcing the ecclesiastical council which had long been promised. He came also, with a large retinue, to Wittenberg and invited Luther to visit him. When they came to speak of the Council, Luther declared that the opposite party were not in earnest, and that, even if such a convention were brought about, the time would be spent, as was customary, in treating of unnecessary matters, not of faith, justification, and true unity in the Spirit and in faith. Upon this Vergerius turned to his attendants and said: "This man certainly sees the chief point in the whole transaction." Luther added: "We are fully certain—through the Holy Ghost—on all points, and have no need of any Council for ourselves, but desire it for the sake of those wretched people who are oppressed by your tyranny; for you do not know what you believe. But, if you desire it, institute one and, by the help of God, I shall come, even though I knew that you would burn me." This Vergerius, ten years afterwards, became a zealous Lutheran; for when, in the hope of becoming a cardinal, he diligently studied the works of Luther for the purpose of refuting them, he became so fully convinced of the truth that he wrote not against Lutheranism, but against the papacy.

Among the many treatises which Luther prepared in this year the Simple Method of Prayer, addressed to a good friend, is especially worthy of note. It contains brief but excellent directions how to use the first three chief parts of the Catechism in prayer.

How ready Luther was to unite with the Reformed, if this could be done without endangering the sound doctrine, is again apparent from the so-called Wittenberg Concord.— In 1536, a short time before Whitsuntide, several Reformed theologians, among whom was Bucer, were sent to Wittenberg for the purpose of conferring once more with Luther and the other theologians upon the doctrine of the Lord's Supper. In the introductory remarks Luther gave his reasons for hitherto doubting the honest intentions of his opponents, and stated especially to Bucer that if he were not honest in his purpose it would be better to lay aside all thoughts of an agreement, in order that the evil might not become worse, and that posterity might not be doomed to sigh on account of such shams. When Bucer, somewhat disconcerted, gave the assurance that he was upright in his intentions, and sought to excuse past proceedings, Luther insisted that they must publicly recant as unchristian the doctrine of the Lord's Supper which they had hitherto taught, and promise to accept and teach the true doctrine with the Lutheran Church; that they must, without reserve, declare that in the sacrament Christ's body and blood are substantially present in the bread and wine, even though he who administers and he who receives it be unworthy. These points were, with others, drawn up by Melanchthon, and were all signed by the Reformed and Lutheran theologians and publicly read from the pulpit.

A portion of the Reformed party expressed their joy at this agreement; the Swiss, however would not receive it, but published a tract against it. Bucer also soon became vacillating again, and even Melanchthon, and others who agreed with him, secretly gave encouragement to the departure from the sound doctrine, and thus did much injury and caused Luther much sorrow in the last years of his life.

In 1537 the Lutheran princes held a convention in Smalcald, where the articles which Luther had been requested to prepare, were signed and ordered to be presented to the council which had been called. These Smalcald Articles were also adopted by the Lutheran Church as part of her public confessions.— Luther accompanied the princes to Smalcald, and there delivered several very important sermons on the three articles of the Christian faith and on Matt. iv, in which he presented a brief view of the whole history of the Church, showing what the Church of Christ, like Christ himself and every individual Christian, must suffer at the hands of Satan, especially how he, as a black devil, in the first three centuries tempted Christians, by external tyranny, to fall away from Christ, and when this failed how he, as a white devil, falsely appealing to the Holy Scriptures, troubled them with various heresies, especially the Arian, and, finally, how he, as a divine devil, induced them under the papacy, to worship him by self-imposed works and services, but how, in the Reformation, the divine mask was torn from Him by the word of God, and he was deprived of all power over those who believe this word.

Whilst he was sojourning at Smalcald Luther suffered intense pain from an attack of the gravel, so that he and others saw death staring him in the face. All the princes and lords who were there, visited him; and when the pious elector approached his bed of suffering, Luther prophetically told him that after his death there would be a division in the university at Wittenberg and that his doctrine would be altered; for even then Melanchthon was suspected of being easily drawn from the rigid truth through a false love of peace.— The elector, who was much concerned on account of Luther's words, declared with firmness that although the prosperity of the university was attributed to Melanchthon's learning and fame, he would rather be deprived of his services than have the truth suffer, even if the university should thus be destroyed. He then comforted Luther with the words: "Our dear Lord God will have mercy upon us for the sake of His word and His name, and spare your life." When he had said this he turned away, for the tears started in his eyes.

But as his pain became more severe Luther desired to be taken to Wittenberg. According to the wish of the elector he was conveyed thither in his own carriage, which was accompanied by another conveyance bearing such articles as Luther might need on the way. Two court physicians were also ordered to exert all their skill toward his recovery. When he left Smalcald he commended himself to the prayers of the Church and made a brief confession of his Christian faith: "I cling to the Lord Jesus and His word, and in my heart know of no other righteousness than the precious blood of Christ, which graciously cleanses me, and all who believe, from every sin, as this is freely confessed in my books and in the Augsburg Confession." At his departure he called to his friends: "May God fill you with hatred toward the pope!" that is, they should remain unaffected by the papal doctrines, and remain open enemies of the pope's idolatry unto their end. While in the carriage he made his will and prepared himself joyfully to receive the Lord Christ, when He should come to take him to Himself. But the Lord again delivered him, after eleven days of suffering, from all his sickness. This occurred at Tambach, a small village near the Thuringian forest. Therefore, filled with gratitude and praise, he there wrote the words: "This is my Peniel, for here hath the Lord appeared unto me as he blessed and delivered the patriarch when he wrestled with the Lord." When he was asked what remedy had cured him of the gravel, he answered: "Prayer ; for," he said, "in all Christian congregations fervent prayers were offered in my behalf, according to the command of St. James v, 14—15."

In Gotha he was met by the delegates of the Reformed Church, Bucer and Lycosthenes, who were commissioned to proceed to Smalcald to promote the cause of the agreement adopted in the previous year. Although Luther was still weak he invited them to visit him and conversed kindly with them. He told them, among other things, that the best thing for them would be to keep quiet in future, to teach sound doctrine, and to confess frankly: Dear friends, God has permitted us to fall; we have erred ; let us be cautious now, and in future teach aright. Nothing is gained by dissembling, and the consciences of the people cannot be quieted by prevarication. God will call us to a strict account also in regard to our doctrine, and therefore we must yield nothing that is God's. From this whole conversation, as well as from a number of Letters of Luther, it is evident that the Reformed pretence as though Luther had partially accepted their doctrine is unfounded ; for whilst he charitably manifested all possible lenity and hoped for the best, he did not, in doctrine, depart one hair's breadth from his former confession.

Upon Luther's return to Wittenberg in restored health, he again continued zealously to pray, study, lecture and preach. He explained, especially, the farewell addresses of Christ, according to John xiv, 16, which Dr. Creuziger took down and subsequently published. This work Luther himself pronounced his best book, but in profound humility adds: "although I did not make it, but Dr. Creuziger manifested in it his great understanding and industry." Whilst Luther now enjoyed comparative peace from his enemies, and had the gratification to see that they, with all their rage and defiance, accomplished but little, yea, that the number of cities and countries which received the Gospel was constantly increasing, a secret division occurred in 1538 among his own followers, which caused him much anxiety. False teachers arose, who strove to banish the law and the doctrine of good works from the Church entirely, and who desired to lead the people to repentance solely by preaching Christ and Him crucified, on which account they were called Antinomians. But as their originator, John Agricola, refused, when challenged by Luther, to defend his works, which he had published anonymously, Luther was compelled to confute this dangerous error in writings and disputations. To his faithful pupil Matthesius he said at table: "You shall see, if our people retain the sound doctrine, how men will be instigated against this school and Church (of Wittenberg) and will write against them, becoming great heretics and dangerous fanatics."

About this time Luther published a German translation of the three chief symbols, (the Apostolic, Nicene and Athanasian, which form the basis of the Book of Concord,) with a beautiful exposition, in which he treated the doctrine of the Trinity and especially that of the Divinity of Christ, briefly and succinctly. He also wrote an extended commentary on the 51. Psalm, in which he set forth the doctrine of repentance in all its compass so convincingly and so consolingly that this work occupies the first place among the many similar masterpieces of Luther.

In the year 1539 Luther was again compelled to witness how the people, when they were delivered from the bondage of the pope, abused their Christian liberty, and how they became constantly more rude and self-secure, despising the ministers and refusing to heed their rebukes. Luther testified loudly and openly that God would avenge such base ingratitude towards His Holy Word by sending them bodily plagues and strong delusions after his death, which also actually came to pass. He also had the mortification to hear similar complaints of the scandalous lives of ministers, who had left the cloisters indeed, but not the sins which are practiced there.

In April, 1539, a violent enemy of Luther, George, duke of Saxony, departed this life, whose death was hastened by the sudden decease of both the heirs to his throne. This portion of Saxony thus came into the possesion of his brother, duke Henry, who had already introduced the reformation in his dominions, and who now, without delay, had the Gospel preached to his new subjects, the most of whom had ardently desired it without having had the opportunity to hear it. This was done first at Leipzig on Whitsunday, when Luther in particular preached in the presence of the duke. Thus was fulfilled what he had foretold : "I see that duke George does not cease to persecute the word of God, the preaching of that word, and the poor Lutherans; yea, that he becomes worse and worse; but I shall live to see the day when God shall exterminate his whole race, and I shall preach he word of God at Leipzig."

CHAPTER XXIX.
THE LAST YEARS OF LUTHER'S LIFE.

Although Luther felt the burdens of age increasing, he still continued teaching the word of God without growing weary. He gave an extended exposition of the 110. Psalm, setting forth the nature of Christ's kingdom, and especially showing that Christ is our King and High Priest, and that all Christians are by faith lords over their enemies, and spiritual priests. He did this with great power of the Spirit. In the same year appeared the instructive work on the "Church and Councils," in which Luther with great erudition proves from the history of the Church that the general Christian Councils never introduced new articles of faith, but only defended the ancient faith against new errors.

In the year 1540 God again heard the prayer of Luther in a wonderful manner. Melanchthon, in consequence of great depression of mind, had become dangerously ill in Weimar. The elector sent his own carraige to bring Luther in great haste. When he arrived, Melanchthon was lying at the point of death. Luther was greatly alarmed, but immediately turned to his dear Lord in earnest prayer, and appealed to all His promises in Holy Scripture concerning the hearing of prayer. He then took Melanchthon by the hand and said: "Be of good cheer, Philip, you shall not die;" and as he knew the cause of his illness he added: "Although God has reason to destroy, yet he has no pleasure in the death of a sinner, but that he turn from his way and live; He desires life and not death; and since He graciously accepted the greatest sinners that ever lived on earth, Adam and Eve, He will not reject you, Philip, or permit you to perish in your sin and depression. Therefore do not give way to the spirit of melancholy and become your own murderer, but trust in the Lord who can kill and make alive." When Luther thus spoke, Melanchthon revived and rapidly regained his strength.

He himself confessed: "I would have died if I had not been snatched from death by the arrival of Luther." A similar hearing of his prayers Luther experienced on two other occasions, so that he could say: "I have secured the deliverance of our Philip, my Kate, and Myconius from death by prayer."

In the autumn of 1540 Melanchthon went with several theologians to attend at Worms a Conference with the Papists. Luther did not accompany them, but said: "God has given us many good learned men who understand His word and can defend it against the opponents." When he took leave of them he blessed them and addressed to them many words of power, among which were these: "Go in the name of the Lord, as ambassadors of Jesus Christ; cling firmly to the simple word of God, and yield nothing that is Christ's, as ye have no authority to yield." As the opponents at the Conference could advance nothing against the arguments of Melanchthon, they postponed the further discussion until the approaching Diet at Regensburg in the year 1541. There the Papists presented a document, generally called the Regensburg Interim, which was intended to serve as a basis for consultation and also, if possible, for union. But Luther clearly proved, his advice having been asked upon the matter, that the purpose of the opponents, especially in regard to the article of Justification, was nothing else than to put a new piece of cloth upon an old garment, whereby the rent would merely be made worse. Matt. ix, 16. A number of foreign princes however, resolved, with the knowledge of the emperor, to send a respectable embassy to Luther, in the hope that he might still be prevailed upon to form an agreement. This resolution was carried into effect, and to the oral address of the ambassadors Luther immediately gave an oral answer, which he subsequently reduced to writing and the import of which was that if the first four articles, especially that concerning Justification, should in all respects be preached purely and be received as Christian, the poison of the other ten would be neutralized, and the clear teachings of these articles and their application by means of correct preaching would soon lead to an agreement in regard to the last ten. Seckendorf, in his excellent History of Lutheranism, praises the answer of Luther in this transaction, which is one of the most important in the Reformation, both for the modesty of its style and and the firmness which it evinced. For as Luther before could not be intimidated by the menaces of Cajetan at Augsburg and of the emperor at Worms, neither could he now be lured to a sinful compliance by the flatteries of such an imposing embassy. But the opponents took no notice of this answer, and again referred the whole matter to a general Council. If the princes and theologians had taken this answer of Luther as their model in the negotiations respecting the Interim, which was, shortly after Luther's death, fabricated from that of Regensburg, the Lutheran Church would not have been so sorely troubled.

At this period Luther suffered manifold bodily pains and infirmities, on which account he was much occupied with thoughts of death and prayed without ceasing for a happy end. He was thus much impeded in his labors, and several times he was compelled to leave the pulpit without finishing his sermon. Frequently he could not read a letter, sometimes not even two or three lines, without resting. Still he wrote a number of excellent works. Besides the beautiful exposition of the Songs of Degrees (Ps. cxx—cxxxv,) he published the two sermons on Matt. iii, concerning the Baptism of Christ and Christians, which he had delivered at the court of Dessau upon the occasion of a prince's baptism. To the ministers he issued an earnest admonition to preach against usury, which, he says, prevailed to such an extent that he scarcely hoped for any amendment. At this period also he published the admirable exposition of the xc. Psalm.

In 1542 Luther consecrated Nicholas von Amsdorf, whom the elector had chosen as Lutheran bishop of Naumburg and Zeitz, and solemnly installed him, on which occasion he preached on an Example of the Consecration of a true Christian Bishop. This sermon he expanded in a work with the same title which was published soon afterwards.

In this year the Bohemian brethren, as their bishop Comenius relates, sent to Luther two delegates, for the fourth and last time, for the purpose of ascertaining what might be expected of the Lutherans in regard to Church discipline. After they had held a friendly conference with him and the other theologians, he invited them to a parting meal, extended his hand to them in the presence of the professors assembled, and said: "Be ye apostles of the Bohemians, and I and my friends will be apostles of the Germans. Perform the work of Christ among your people, as you shall have opportunity, and we will do it among ours according to the ability given us." Luther's manner of conducting the work of the Lord was to provide the Church first of all with the pure doctrine, that the true faith might be planted and nurtured as a good tree, showing constantly how such a tree must of itself bear the fruits of a holy life, at the same time using all his endeavors, in his works and by his counsels, as circumstances required, to introduce good external discipline, of which all the Lutheran Church constitutions of the period of the Reformation bear ample testimony.

Towards the close of the year 1543, Luther had the pleasure of receiving a lengthy communication from several brethren in Italy, who had been led to a knowledge of the truth by his writings. This indicated an unutterable joy in the treasure of sound doctrine, a fervent zeal for its preservation, a resolute rejection of all error, particularly in regard to the sacramental controversy, a firm steadfastness amid all persecutions, a profound reverence for the chosen instrument Luther, and a high appreciation of his works, which was based upon their own experience. As a specimen of this laudable epistle, the whole of which would occupy too much space, we transcribe the first sentence, which reads thus: "The rivers of living water which flow from thee, reverend Sir, must be swollen more and more by the heavenly rains with which it shall be your task to water the thirsty pastures of the Lord, as well there by daily sermons as here by your writings." The joy of these honest people must have been great when they received the excellent answer of Luther, in which he paternally warns them particularly against the sacramentarians.

In 1543 the Lutheran Church was again beset by various dangers, including some from without. But Luther in these also manifested a strong confidence in his God, and foretold with full assurance that there would be no war during his life.

When Caspar Schwenkfeld, who endeavored to put a new dress upon the old errors of the sacramentarians, and thus deceived many persons in Silesia, sent several of his tracts to Luther, the latter replied to him in the severe words which he merited, telling him plainly: "Leave me unmolested with the books which the devil spues from you." The same zeal against false doctrine Luther manifested at that period in another similar case. When a publisher sent him a Swiss translation of the Bible, he wrote to him that he should keep his present, because it was a work of his preachers, with whom, inasmuch as they refused to renounce their error, he could have no fellowship.

Luther also, in a number of publications, refuted the enemies of Christianity who were outside of the Church. He republished in the German language a refutation of the Koran, the religious book of the Turks, and in the preface earnestly warned against such satanic doctrine. In the year 1543 he wrote a number of books against the Jews, in which he cleared many beautiful texts of the lies with which they had perverted them, and exposed their blasphemous and diabolical malice against Christ and his disciples. Nor did he now, as he had done formerly, believe in a future general conversion of the Jews. Finally, in this year also appeared the important work on the Last Words of David (2 Sam. xxiii, 1—7,) in which he earnestly and forcibly treats of the Three Persons in the Holy Trinity and the two Natures in the one undivided Person of the Lord Christ, so that by this powerful treatise every Christian may be established in his faith and guarded against all kinds of error.

Notwithstanding that Luther with advancing age experienced increasing ailments in his mortal frame, he still unweariedly participated in the whole work of the Reformation; and whilst he, as a true watchman upon the walls of Zion, was always on the alert, his ardent zeal for the preservation of sound doctrine induced him to write a number of works, especially against the sacramentarians. Schwenkfeld, notwithstanding the severe rebuke which he had received, with incredible hardihood still pretended that Luther harmonized with him. This induced the latter in 1544 to publish the book entitled, "Brief Confession on the Lord's Supper against the Fanatics," of which he himself says: "I, who stand on the verge of the grave, shall take this testimony and glory with me to the judgment seat of my dear Lord and Savior Jesus Christ, that I have with all earnestness condemned and avoided the fanatics and foes of the sacrament, Carlstadt, Zwingli, Œcolampadius, Stenkfeld, and their disciples at Zurich, or wherever they may be, and our preaching, as they well know, is daily directed against their blasphemous and slanderous heresy."

In the year 1545 Melanchthon, with a view of laying it before the Diet of Worms, drew up the so-called Wittenberg Opinion concerning the Reformation, which Luther also signed, upon which occasion he testified that it is impossible to remain faithful to the Word of God and preserve a conscience void of offence, and at the same time retain the favor of the world and receive credit for gentleness.

It was Luther's lot to experience yet, a short time before his death, the bitterest sorrows, inasmuch as, especially in Wittenberg, ungodliness of life caused one scandal after another, which tortured his soul and finally induced him, in 1545, to depart from the city and visit his friends at Merseburg and Zeitz. But the elector, to whom the university had earnestly represented the matter, addressed to him a very gracious letter, in which he promised to do all in his power to remove the evils, thus inducing him to return to Wittenberg.— There he completed the sixth and last edition of his German Bible, at the improvement of which he and his learned friends had been constantly laboring, inserting many beautiful observations which are known by the name "of marginal notes." He also finished one of his greatest masterpieces, the large Commentary on Genesis, upon which he had lectured, although with frequent interruptions, for the previous ten years. Finally he published also the earnest and energetic work: "The Papacy instituted by the Devil," which was his last book.

According to the command of the emperor another religious conference between the contending parties was to be held in the early part of the year 1546, to which Dr. Major was sent from Wittenberg. When he went to Luther to take leave of him, he found at the entrance of his study the words written in Luther's hand: "Our professors are to be examined on the Lord's Supper."

CHAPTER XXX.

LUTHER'S LAST DAYS, DEATH AND BURIAL.

In one of his last sermons Luther exhorted his hearers to pray diligently and to prove the spirits, and, when they should hear of his being sick, not to pray that his life might be prolonged, but that a happy end might be granted him. "I am weary of the world," he said, "and the world of me; it is therefore easy to part, as when a guest quits his lodgings."

Luther's last sermon delivered in Wittenberg, Jan. 17., on Rom. xii. 3, is also remarkable, in which he treats of the fruits of faith in Christ and of reason and its conceit, and in which he says: "We can notice usury, drunkenness, adultery, murder, &c., and the world also knows them to be sin; but Satan's bride, reason, the pretty strumpet, walks abroad in boasted wisdom and what she says she thinks is of the Holy Spirit: who is to help us here? No jurist, physician or king can render us assistance. For she is the greatest harlot that Satan has. Other gross sins can be seen; but reason can be judged by no man; she introduces fanaticism respecting Baptism and the Lord's Supper, and thinks that whatever Satan suggests to her must be the Holy Spirit. Therefore St. Paul says: 'As I am an apostle and have received the Spirit, I exhort you.'"

In this sermon Luther also foretold the troubles which came upon the Lutheran Church shortly after his death. He says: "I plainly see that, unless God gives us faithful ministers of the Church, Satan will rend our churches by means of the sectarian fanatics and will not cease until he has accomplished his end. This is his purpose, and if he cannot effect it through the pope and the emperor, he will do it through those who are not yet agreed with us in doctrine. Therefore it is necessary for us to pray that God would give us pure teachers. At present we feel secure and see not how terribly the prince of this world seeks to ensnare us by means of the pope, the emperor, and our learned men of this place, whilst we say: What harm can it do if we yield this? No, not a hair's breadth dare we yield. If they agree with us, well; if they will not, they must let it alone. I have not received the doctrine from them, but by divine grace from God. I am well advised. Therefore earnestly pray God that ye may retain His word, for perilous times are approaching." The publisher of this sermon observes at the close with regard to the Wittenberg University: "Dr. Martin Luther, of blessed memory, often remarked in the hearing of Dr. Augustine Schurf and other credible persons: 'After my death none of these theologians will remain steadfast.' And this, alas! has proved true."

In the autumn of the previous year Luther had, at the request of the count of Mansfeld, journeyed to Eisleben for the purpose of effecting an agreement between the counts and their subjects, whom they sought to deprive of their mines. Having then failed to accomplish his end, he set out again for the same purpose in the beginning of the year 1546. He himself said that he had, upon the invitation of the counts of Mansfeld, left Wittenberg in order to be free from his daily toil and trouble, and to devote himself to prayer, preaching and the restoration of harmony and peace among his rulers. He accordingly set out on the Saturday after his last sermon, Jan. 23., with his three sons, and arrived at Halle on the following Sunday, where he visited his faithful friend Dr. Jonas; and on the following day, being the festival of St. Paul's Conversion, he preached on Acts 9, 1—19 concerning St. Paul's Call to the Apostleship. He especially commended St. Paul's writings as the true relic, in comparison with which all the feigned relics of the pope, particularly the pretended head of St. Paul which was exhibited at St. Peter's in Rome, are to be regarded as nothing.

After he had, with great peril, crossed the Saale near Halle in a boat, and had, on the borders of the Mansfeld territory, been received by the counts and upwards of a hundred horsemen, he was escorted to Eisleben. A short distance from the city he became so unwell that his life was considered in danger. But he became better and tarried three weeks in Eisleben, taking part in the negotiations until the day before his death. His efforts to restore harmony were again baffled by the jurists, so that Luther determined, if his life were spared, to write a book against them. During his stay at Eisleben he ordained two ministers and twice received absolution and the Holy Supper. He also preached four sermons, as he was always very diligent in preaching, making the statement himself that he often delivered four sermons in one day and did this for twenty-five years. In these four sermons Luther, notwithstanding his bodily weakness, bore the most powerful testimony to all the chief articles of the Christian faith and against all the errors of the Papists, Sacramentarians and other fanatics.

At the close of his last sermon, three days before his death, he took formal leave of his dear friends at Eisleben and said: "As I have now been here some time and preached to you, and must now return home and perhaps shall preach no more, I would now bless you and entreat you to adhere steadfastly to the Word which your ministers by the grace of God faithfully teach you, and to cultivate the habit of praying that God would protect you against all the wise and prudent who despise the doctrine of the Gospel, since they have done much injury and might do more." He then concluded his last sermon with the words: "May God grant us His grace that we may with gratitude receive His word, increase in the knowledge and faith of His Son, our Lord

Jesus Christ, and firmly abide in the confession of His blessed word to the end. Amen."

As he was accustomed to do always, he prayed with great fervor every evening in his room at the open window, after which he returned joyfully to his friends, like one who had been relieved of a heavy burden, and conversed with them for half an hour before retiring to rest. In these last days of his life many important remarks and words of comfort fell from his lips at table. On February 17. his weakness increased visibly, so that he was advised to take rest, which he also did. On the last evening, among other things, he answered the question whether believers would know each other in the future world, by adducing the case of Adam, who immediately knew his wife to be bone of his bone and flesh of his flesh, because he was full of the Holy Ghost and of the knowledge of God. He then went to his room and prayed, as was his custom, especially for the Church of his native land, but soon afterwards complained of an oppressive sensation in the breast. He took the medicine which was given him and, at about 8 o'clock, laid himself upon his couch, saying: "If I could slumber a half hour it would, I hope, become better." He then slept quietly until 10 o'clock, when he awoke and arose, saying as he entered his bed-room: "In the name of God I retire to rest; into Thy hands I commit my spirit; Thou hast redeemed me, Lord God of truth." When he had retired to bed he extended his hand to all, bade them good night, and said: "Dr. Jonas and M. Cœlius and the rest of you, pray for our Lord God and His Gospel, that it may prosper; for the Council of Trent and the odious pope are greatly enraged against it."

As the clock struck one he awoke and said: "O Lord God, how ill I feel! Ah, dear Dr. Jonas, I believe I shall remain here at Eisleben, where I was born and baptized." He then went from his chamber to the room and repeated: "Into Thy hands I commend my spirit; Thou hast redeemed me, Lord God of truth." When perspiration had been produced by rubbing him with warm cloths, and his friends, especially the counts who had come in haste to visit him, expressed the hope that his condition would now improve, he said: "Yes, it is the cold sweat of death; I shall yield up my spirit, for the sickness grows worse." He then prayed in these words: "O my heavenly Father, the God and Father of our Lord Jesus Christ, Thou God of all consolation, I thank Thee that Thou hast revealed to me Thy dear Son Jesus Christ, in whom I believe, whom I have preached and confessed, whom I have loved and extolled, whom the pernicious pope and all the ungodly dishonor, persecute and blaspheme. I pray Thee, Lord Jesus Christ, receive my soul into Thy care. O heavenly Father, although I must leave this body and be torn away from this life, I nevertheless know assuredly that I shall be with Thee forever and that no one can pluck me out of Thy hands."

He also said further in Latin: "God so loved the world that He gave His only begotten Son, that whosoever believeth in Him should not perish, but have everlasting life," John 3, 16; and the words of the 68. Psalm: "He that is our God is the God of salvation, and unto God the Lord belong the issues from death." A physician having offered him a tonic, he took it and again said: "I pass away, I shall yield up my spirit," after which he rapidly thrice repeated the words in Latin: "Father, into Thy hands I commend my spirit; Thou hast redeemed me, Lord God of truth." He then lay quietly with folded hands and closed eyes. His friends spoke to him, but he returned no answer. Upon this Jonas and Cœlius addressed to him in loud tones the question: "Reverend father, are you willing to die in firm adherence to Christ and the doctrine which you have preached?" to which he answered so distinctly that all could hear it: "Yes." This was his last word. Having uttered this he turned upon his right side and slept about a quarter of an hour. Some of those present again began to entertain hopes of his recovery, when his face became deathly pale; his hands and feet became cold; he drew one more deep, gentle breath, and yielded up his spirit into the hands of his faithful God in quiet resignation. He thus fell asleep, in the Lord, gently and peacefully,

12*

after a last illness of only about seven hours, without disquietude, without pains of body or pangs of death, on the 18th of February, 1546, between two and three o'clock in the morning, in the 63rd year of his pilgrimage on earth.

The sad tidings of Luther's death rapidly spread through town and country. A large multitude of persons of all classes came to view the corpse while burning tears ran down their cheeks. Early on the 19th of February the letters announcing Luther's death reached Wittenberg and caused general consternation and profound sorrow. Melanchthon was charged by the professors with communicating the painful intelligence to the students. He did this in a brief Latin address, citing the words of Elisha (2 K. 2, 12), which he had also previously applied to him: "Alas! he has been taken from us, the chariot of Israel and the horsemen thereof, by whom the Church was led in this last age of the world." The funeral of Luther was truly princely. On February 19. the corpse was laid in a metallic coffin and borne amidst the singing of hymns to the principal Church of Eisleben, where it was placed before the altar, while Dr. Jonas preached a funeral sermon on 1 Thess. 4, 13–18, treating of the person and gifts of Dr. Luther, of the resurrection and eternal life, and of the power against the kingdom of Satan which his death leaves to us. In the evening the elector's answer to the reports which had been sent to him was received, according to which the corpse was to be brought to Wittenberg for burial. On the following day, February 20., the minister at Eisleben, M. Cœlius, delivered an excellent funeral sermon on Is. 57, 1–2, after which the corpse was with great solemnity removed from Eisleben. An innumerable multitude surrounded the hearse with weeping and mourning, and in nearly all the villages the bells were tolled.

When the corpse, late in the evening, arrived at the gates of Halle, it was received with great honors and brought to the church while Luther's hymn: "From deep distress to Thee I cry," was sobbed rather than sung. On the next day the corpse was conveyed further on its way, was everywhere received with solemnity and escorted, and finally reached Wittenberg on the 22. of February. Here the funeral procession moved, amid singing and the tolling of all the bells, to the castle church in the following order. First came the school choirs and the ministers, followed by the commissaries of the elector and the counts of Mansfeld with a train of 60 horsemen. Next came the hearse, drawn by four horses, covered with a large costly pall of black velvet, the gift of the elector. Then followed Luther's widow and his three children and other relatives; next the Rector of the University in his official robe, accompanied by princes and nobles who were studying there. These were followed by the professors, the city council, the students and the citizens. When the corpse had been brought into the Church Dr. Bugenhagen preached a consolatory sermon on 1 Thess. 4, 13–14, in the delivery of which he was frequently interrupted by his own tears and those of his hearers. In conclusion Melanchthon delivered a Latin address, after which the corpse was lowered into the grave near the pulpit, upon which Luther had preached so many powerful sermons, and was thus, as St. Paul says, sown in weakness, that it might arise on that day to eternal glory.

May our heavenly Father, who called Luther to this great work, our Lord Jesus Christ, whom he faithfully preached and confessed, and the Holy Spirit, who by His Divine power gave him such cheerfulness and confidence against the gates of hell in so many mighty conflicts, help us all, that we may attain the same peaceful departure from this life to the same eternal blessedness.

In conclusion, my dear readers, I address to you the words of Hebr. 13, 7: "Remember them which have the rule over you, who have spoken unto you the word of God: whose faith follow, considering the end of their conversation."

The hero now enjoys a peaceful rest,
   Through whom the Lord has great deliv'rance wrought,
   From all the falsehoods which the pope had taught,
And with the light of truth our souls has blest.
But we must still abide the battle's test.
   The latter days approach with terror fraught,
   The roaring waves impel to serious thought.
O, that we all might heed the Lord's behest,
   Error to shun, for His own truth contend,
   And, holding fast this treasure to the end,
Confess it steadfastly to all around,
   Nor swerve one hair's breadth from the heavenly line.
   O God! fill us for this with grace divine,
That we among the faithful may be found.

www.ingramcontent.com/pod-product-compliance
Lightning Source LLC
Chambersburg PA
CBHW020828190426
43197CB00037B/732